THE BEATLES

An Illustrated Record

ROY CARR & TONY TYLER

HARMONY BOOKS
a division of Crown Publishers, Inc.
419 Park Avenue South
New York, New York 10016

Acknowledgements

Alan Warner John Bagnall Derek Taylor Pam Eaton Jonh Ingham
Sue Humphries Tony King Nick Logan Howard Mylett Bernard White

The authors: Roy Carr (left) and Tony Tyler (right).

The authors would like to thank the persons and organisations
listed below for their help with this book, and to express
a particular debt of gratitude to those pictured above.

Fiona Foulger, Margo Stevens, Shirley Natanson, Moira Bellas,
Andrew Lauder, Tony Brainsby, Sue Dunkley, Louis Raynor,
Joe Pope's Strawberry Fields Forever Society,
Chris Poole, Percy Dickins, Andy Gray, Millie and Pauline
Sutcliffe, Risa Rosenthal, Pennie Smith, Bleecker Bob's Village Oldies
(New York), Stephen F. D. Baker, Helmuth Ungar,
Lon Goddard, Mike and Pete – the Vintage Record Centre (London),
The Golden Disc (New York), Apple Records, ATV, DJM Records,
Decca Records, EMI Records, Atlantic Records, Virgin Records,
Disc, Fab 208, Bill Harry, Ted's 'Rock On' Record
Stall (London), Tony Stewart, Greg Shaw's 'Who Put the Bomp' –
and, of course, the fabled archives of 'New Musical Express'.

Thanks are also due to the following for providing illustrations
for this book: Apple, Anglo-EMI, Associated Press, ATV Network,
Camera Press, Tedd Church, Richard Creamer, Richard Dilello,
Robert Ellis, EMI, Epoque Ltd., Fox Photos, Bob Gruen, Tom
Hanley, Dezo Hoffmann, Keystone Press Agency, King Features –
Subafilms, Bob Lampard, London Photo Agency, Doug Luke, Mirrorpic,
Orbit Press Features, Bent Reg, Rex
Features Ltd., SKR Photos, Joseph Stevens, Syndication
International, United Press International.

Published by Harmony Books
A Division of Crown Publishers Inc.
419 Park Avenue South, New York, NY 10016

First published 1975. Reprinted 1975

Created and Produced by
Trewin Copplestone Publishing Ltd
Design and text © Trewin Copplestone Publishing Ltd, 1975

Published simultaneously in Canada by General Publishing
Company Ltd.

Filmsetting by Filmtype Services Limited, Scarborough
Origination by Metric Reproductions Ltd, Chelmsford
Printed in England by Ben Johnson and Co. Ltd, York
ISBN 0-517-520-451

Library of Congress Catalog Card Number: 74-32652

Contents

THE INTRO...

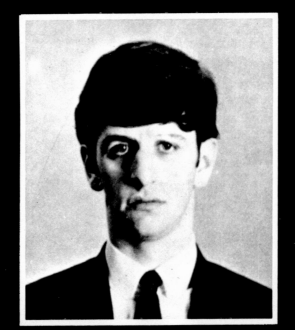

When John Lennon first met Paul McCartney both were about fourteen and John was mildly inebriated. 'He kept putting his arm around my shoulders', recalls McCartney. 'His breath smelt but I showed him a few chords he didn't know. I left feeling I'd created an impression.'

Legends have been woven from humbler stuff, but this particular encounter between two loutish Liverpool schoolboys in the late 'fifties led to events that shook the world.

This is no exaggeration. How many of us can look around and deny that the Beatles at least *seemed* to initiate many of those changes in our social attitudes and tastes that took place in the 'sixties and which still reverberate today? Possibly it was just the group's good luck to be so closely identified with these mass changes in consciousness. Yet many who still view the whole Beatle Phenomenon through wistfully pink-lensed spectacles will *always* secretly be convinced that the Beatles were behind the whole thing from the start.

The Beatles' creative career can be discerned – with hindsight – as a series of periods interspersed with hiatuses of consolidation and/or hesitancy. These are roughly as follows. Firstly, the Early Years, from school groups to professional status, through the prized recording contract (1962) to national recognition. Secondly, Beatlemania, from national to international acclaim to riots and withdrawal from public appearances. Thirdly, the Studio Years, the period when the Beatles became openly and wildly eclectic, producing a matchless series of 'studio' LPs; and finally, the Solo Years, dating from the informal and then formal break-up of the group, and including the great number of individual LPs produced since that time. (The comprehensive survey of recordings which forms the major part of the book is divided into four sections corresponding to these 'natural breaks', while the period before the recording contract is dealt with in the following text.)

It is popularly imagined that all four Beatles are products of Liverpool working-class backgrounds; this is not so. The picture is essentially one of alert, lower-middle-class youths coming into contact with a more virile and exotic – and certainly less 'acceptable' – culture, and reacting sharply and instantly to its influences. Only Ringo Starr is a genuine product of those picturesquely crumbling slums beloved of *Life* magazine photographers.

If John's school group the Quarrymen (who were playing at the garden fête where the meeting described in the first paragraph actually took place) are to be considered the first incarnation of the Beatles, then it is probably because this strictly amateur outfit provided the first instance when John Lennon, Paul McCartney and George Harrison actually played together.

The earlier group had primitive equipment and only rudimentary expertise: the addition of Paul provided a somewhat more talented guitarist, and the later inclusion of George (a schoolfriend of McCartney's) added a still-better player.

They were strictly a school group and, in 1959, all three left their respective academies. But John, Paul and George, each with a proper guitar and a strong desire to continue playing, stayed together. But three soloists and no rhythm is not (and never was) an acceptable formula for success: a drummer and bassist were required, and immediately, if the Quarrymen – as they still called themselves – were to progress.

Lennon was then attending Liverpool College of Art, where he had fallen in with a certain Stuart Sutcliffe, a talented painter and a natural stylist with a great flair for image cultivation. Lennon admired Sutcliffe intensely and wanted him in the group – so when Stu happened upon an unexpected £60 fee for some paintings, the hustling Lennon swiftly pointed out his golden opportunity to buy into the band . . . for the price of a bass guitar, a mere, er . . . £60 or so. He couldn't play? They'd teach him. Sutcliffe bought the bass and duly joined the group but kept his back to the audience for the first months in perpetual terror lest some

Top *A pre-teen George, already guitar-minded.*

Above *A studious young John.*

Left *Immortalisation of John's twenty-five yards in a Liverpool swimming pool.*

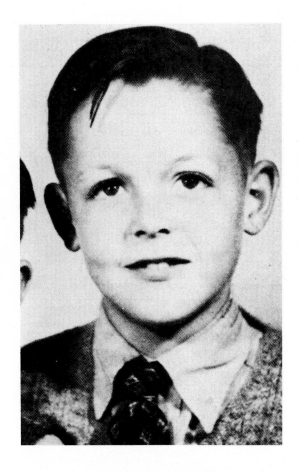

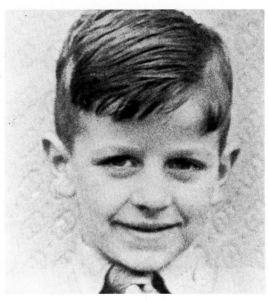

Top *Paul aged nine.*

Above *Ringo, slightly younger.*

Above right *John with Auntie Mimi.*

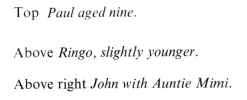

expert in the audience detect his lack of ability.

The provision of a drummer was a more serious matter. They were badly let down by a stand-in for a vital Larry Parnes audition; another audition candidate, the locally prestigious Johnny Hutchinson, stood in instead. Parnes, a well-known impresario, declined to offer them the Billy Fury backing-band engagement he was auditioning – but was sufficiently impressed to send the embryonic group to Scotland on a short tour supporting another Parnes' artist, Johnny Gentle. They were now professional, and to prove it, hired a drummer, one Thomas Moore. They called themselves the Silver Beatles (taking vainglorious stage names – Paul *Ramon*, Johnny *Silver*, Stu *de Stijl* and *Carl* Harrison – and Thomas Moore) and proceeded on their first proper tour, of which they now remember little or nothing.

The picture is now of five proudly professional, decidedly ambitious young men, becoming popular in their own environs – and even some distance afield.

The drummer problem was at this stage solved by Peter Best, introverted son of Mrs Best, owner of the Casbah club, being recruited into the group. They had all known Best for some time; the Quarrymen had actually opened the Casbah in the first place, and it had later been one of their regular engagements (at fifteen shillings a night). Pete, encouraged by his mother to take an interest in running the club, had also acquired a drum kit. When the Silver Beatles came back from Scotland – goodbye to Thomas Moore, who thus disappears from our history – they were almost immediately offered a residency in Hamburg, the first of the five famous residencies in that city which were to teach them the endurance and on-stage extroversion which later played such a large part in their initial impact.

7

Above *An interesting double exposure of Stuart Sutcliffe.*

Top *At Arnhem War Cemetery, en route for Hamburg, 1960. Left to right: 'Lord Woodbine', Liverpool strip-club owner Stuart Sutcliffe, Paul, George and Pete Best. John is not in evidence – he was taking the picture.*

Hamburg's Indra Club required a group with a drummer; Best was found suitable. Off they drove, having their pictures taken at Arnhem War Cemetery on the way. The Indra proved a scruffy establishment, but the local hoodlums delighted in wild on-stage antics, and the aloof stage personas of the Silver Beatles vanished with the need to 'Make *Schau*', as the club-owner demanded.

A fairly murky period of squabbling and cockiness follows. Perhaps the enthusiastic receptions that late-night Hamburg strollers gave their sets encouraged them to progress from mock violence to real (attempted) acts of aggression and outrage. The story has been told of how John and Pete Best set fire to the wallpaper in their dingy accommodation (which actually seems a perfectly reasonable action under the circumstances). Lennon later confessed that they'd also once tried to 'roll' a drunken English sailor, but had been overcome with self-contempt, abandoning the project. For the wallpaper incident John and Pete were deported, one day after George was similarly 'asked to leave' because of his age (seventeen), below the minimum (eighteen) required by West German law for public performance in bars and clubs.

They returned to Liverpool already a much better band. Eight hours on stage – with a further four on standby – reinforces both inventiveness and stamina, and their voices were already rawer and cruder from the strain. In their absence, the Casbah had mushroomed in popularity, and the Beatles – as they now were – played many dates there, gaining new fans. They also played several of Liverpool's more prestigious venues: Litherland Town Hall saw their most successful Liverpool concert to date, and they shortly began gigging at the famous Cavern Club, a Dixieland haven originally designed as a warehouse and open throughout the 'fifties for trad jazz nights.

From the Cavern back to Hamburg and the appearance of the Beatle haircut; the departure

Above *Left to right: Klaus Voormann, Astrid Kirchherr and Stuart Sutcliffe.*

Left *Hamburg, 1960. Left to right: George, Stuart Sutcliffe and John.*

Top *With Pete Best (centre) at the Cavern.*

9

of Stu Sutcliffe, and their first recordings – under the *aegis* of Bert Kaempfert – as backing musicians for singer Tony Sheridan.

The origins of the haircuts are unclear. Some say they came about as a direct result of the influence of Astrid Kirchherr and her circle of friends, which included Klaus Voormann. Oddly enough, a similar hairstyle was being adopted at the time throughout Liverpool Art College, where it was – deprecatingly – known as a 'Julius Caesar'.

This second Hamburg visit was played at the more prestigious Kaiserkeller club. Shortly after the group arrived in Hamburg to take up the engagement, Stu informed the others that he'd decided to leave – to remain in Hamburg with Astrid and study painting. They agreed, since Paul was already a much better player and would be more economically employed on bass than on second lead-guitar. They finished their residency and returned to Liverpool. Nine months after they did so, Sutcliffe collapsed and died of a brain haemorrhage.

In Liverpool they continued to play crowd-pulling concerts, at the Cavern and Litherland Town Hall and New Brighton Tower among other places. The *Liverpool Echo* failed to notice the existence of the Mersey Beat Boom – of which the Beatles were only a part – so what was virtually an 'underground' paper, *Mersey Beat*, was launched by ex-Liverpool University Rag Mag editor Bill Harry – incidentally, a man who can justifiably claim to have done a great deal for the Beatles' early career.

So could Brian Epstein. It was between the Beatles' second and third Hamburg visits that a certain Raymond Jones strolled into NEMS, Epstein's Whitechapel record store, and asked for 'My Bonnie' by Tony Sheridan and the Beatles. Mystified that a Liverpool group should have a following of any sort, Epstein hunted them down . . . at the Cavern. It was November 9, 1961, and the club was, as he later wrote, 'Dark, damp and smelly. And I regretted my decision immediately. The noise was deafening.'

But he signed them anyway, after more careful study. 'He [Epstein] looked efficient and rich', remembers John.

Epstein had little time to do other than arrange contracts, set up NEMS Enterprises and arrange a premature (and non-productive) Decca Records audition before the Beatles flew back to Hamburg for their third 'European Tour'. This time they were to guest at the newly opened Star Club in Hamburg's Grosse Freiheit, clearly destined to be the city's leading *rockhaus*. The Star was owned by plutocrat Manfred Weissleder – but run by the small and energetic Horst Fascher, a shrewd ex-lightweight boxer with a killer punch and disarming charm. Fascher was fascinated by the Beatles' eating habits ('Cornflakes. Always cornflakes'), but on paydays the group ate at the Seamen's Mission, dining regally on steak, chips, eggs and pints of fresh milk. Fascher's other skills came in useful within the Star Club's precincts, where drunken sailors clashed nightly with ferocious bouncers armed with gas-pistols and rubber coshes. This aggravation fired up the Beatles' act even more – but it also fed their growing impatience to get decisively ahead with their careers.

Then . . . a telegram arrived from Epstein announcing they'd won an EMI Records audition. They returned to Liverpool in the due course of events, travelled down to London and went through their paces for EMI A & R man George Martin, who kept politely poker-faced throughout the proceedings.

But they still had a further waiting period – while they won *Mersey Beat* polls and sold out dances all over West Lancashire. At the end of July 1962 Martin manoeuvred a Parlophone Records contract for the delighted Beatles. On August 16 an ashen-faced Pete Best was sacked from the group.

Best was struck numb, but his many fans were hotly partisan, and George – who'd argued most strongly for Best's replacement – was punched in the eye by one of them. The man who took the new job was Richard Starkey (stage-name Ringo Starr) formerly an alumnus of Rory Storme and the Hurricanes and a veteran of Butlin's Holiday Camps, US Air Force bases and Hamburg.

Ringo had taken a sabbatical from Storme to play in the Star Band (the Hamburg club's house outfit, fronted by Tony Sheridan), and so met the Beatles on their third visit. Sometime between the arrival of Epstein's telegram and the EMI audition the decision was taken – between John, Paul and, notably, George – to oust Pete Best. Ringo, faced with a further season at Butlin's or a permanent job with the Beatles, wisely chose the latter, somehow managing to avoid the fury that temporarily descended upon the remaining three from Best supporters.

Though the matter was badly handled – Best was unnecessarily humiliated and betrayed – the change in personnel (the first for reasons of *policy*) hardly affected the Beatles' status as Liverpool Kings. While impatiently awaiting Martin to communicate an actual date for recording, they spent their time having their pictures taken in Liverpool's main music store, taking delivery of matching Gibson jumbo guitars. (The store hung the photo till it yellowed.) The *Liverpool Echo* had begun to notice them, in a vague sort of way. And – most important – they actually possessed a real recording contract and were going to make a record.

On September 11, 1962, the Beatles went down to London, to record 'Love Me Do' at the EMI studios. Clutching their guitars, they were shown into the studio by George Martin. 'Let me know if there's anything you don't like', he told them. 'For a start', said George Harrison, 'I don't like your tie.'

Top *Ringo at Butlins. This period of his life was later re-lived by him in the film 'That'll Be the Day'.*

Above *Still at the Cavern.*

Left *Paul and John with Gene Vincent at the Cavern.*

11

MERSEYSIDE'S OWN ENTERTAINMENTS PAPER

MERSEY BEAT

Vol. 1 No. 13   JANUARY 4-18, 1962   Price **THREEPENCE**

Beatles Top Poll!

FULL RESULTS INSIDE

Cover photograph by Albert Marrion

JOHN LENNON   GEORGE HARRISON   PAUL McARTREY   PETE BEST

The Early Years

Left *Top of the* Mersey Beat *polls, but still waiting for the prized recording contract, and still in their scruffy attire. Above* Late 1962, *and our heroes have both the contract and new suits, but their rather stiff and awkward poses demonstrate an understandable feeling of insecurity.*

1962

January 1
Beatles ring in the New Year by auditioning for Decca Records in London. George sings 'The Sheik of Araby', Paul 'Red Sails in the Sunset' and John 'Please Mr Postman'. Decca A&R man Mike Smith whoops 'terrific', but his superior Dick Rowe disagrees. Decca sign Brian Poole and the Tremoloes.

'Groups of guitars are on the way out. Mr Epstein — you really should stick to selling records in Liverpool.'
Decca A & R Man Dick Rowe.

January/May
Beatles back at the Star Club, drowning their sorrows and polishing up their act.

April 10
Stuart Sutcliffe, The Beatles' ex-bassist, dies suddenly in Hamburg at the age of twenty-one of a brain tumour.

Above left *Enter George Martin, future Beatles' record producer.*

Above *John at the first recording session.*

Far Left *Stuart Sutcliffe photographed in Hamburg shortly before his death.*

Left *Richard Starkey before his translation into Ringo Starr, Beatle.*

'Love Me Do' (Paul)/'P.S. I Love You' (Paul)
Parlophone R 4949. Produced: George Martin
Released: October 5, 1962

In 1962, for a new, virtually unproven group to record a self-composed pair of tracks on their first outing for a national record label was nothing short of foolhardy, especially as, in the derivative British rock tradition, safety lay in 'covering' US-established hits. *'Love, love me do – you know I love you'* were hardly lyrics to break the tried pattern of moon 'n June wordage which had dogged pop music since its early days. And the instrumentation – fairly jaunty, harmonica-based chugalong whimsy – did nothing to expand the frontiers of beat group musicianship. One rhythm guitar, played by George Harrison, kept the pulse going, while Lennon's harmonica provided intro, middle eight solo and outro. Unadventurous indeed. But the near-amateurishness of the product *was* appealing – and the musical structure of the B-side, 'P.S. I Love You', proved that subtle chord-shifts lay well within the new group's repertoire.

The session took place on September 11, 1962. Pete Best was Out, and Ringo Starr was In. But Producer George Martin didn't want to invest too much of EMI's studio time in an untried drummer, so he organised Andy White, a well-known session man, to play the simple drum part; the hapless Ringo was given a tambourine to rattle. 'Love Me Do' took seventeen 'takes' to perfect – and during the course of these attempts the percussionists switched roles. The finished track was chosen from the few that Ringo had contributed.

The single reached the low twenties in the nationwide charts – and, predictably, most of the sales were accounted for by loyal Liverpudlians.

June 6
Beatles pass EMI Audition.

'CONGRATULATIONS BOYS EMI REQUEST RECORDING SESSION PLEASE REHEARSE NEW MATERIAL.' Telegram from Brian Epstein to Beatles in Hamburg.

August
Richard Starkey (Ringo Starr) washes the grease from his hair, bids adieu to Rory Storme's Hurricanes, shaves away facial fungus and signs on the dotted line. Exit Pete Best, fuming.

August 23
John Lennon and Cynthia Powell pledge 'till death us do part' at Liverpool's Mount Pleasant Registry Office.

September
EMI's George Martin signs the Beatles.

October 5
'Love Me Do' Parlophone R 4949.

November
Beatles smile sweetly in their first-ever television appearance – Granada's 'People and Places'.

December
On fifth (and final) trip to Hamburg's Star Club, a banner hung across the Grosse Freiheit proclaims 'Welcome Beatles'.

'Liverpool? You're joking. So what's from Liverpool?' Music Publisher Dick James.

All four Beatles – Ringo is lurking in the background – with George Martin at the EMI studios. History in the making, though no one knew it at the time.

15

1963

February
On first nationwide junket supporting Helen Shapiro, Danny Williams and Kenny Lynch; the Beatles thrown out of sedate Midlands hotel restaurant for attempting to dine in leather jackets.

February 16
'Please Please Me' ensconced at Number One on singles chart.

March
Tommy Roe and Chris Montez find the going rough, touring Britain with these four upstarts from Liverpool.

April 1
New Musical Express Pollwinners concert at Wembley.

May/June
Top of the bill for the very first time – with Roy Orbison and Gerry and the Pacemakers in support.

Above *With Roy Orbison (right), Gerry and the Pacemakers.*

Opposite page *'Please Please Me', UK release.*

16

'Please Please Me' (John)/'Ask Me Why' (John)
Parlophone R 4983. Produced: George Martin
Released: January 12, 1963

Back from Hamburg's Star Club after their fourth visit – contracted before EMI showed interest – they found George Martin anxious to have them record a Mitch Murray composition entitled 'How Do You Do It'. But they refused, John Lennon's being the loudest protest of all. To qualify his obstinacy, he produced another from the Lennon/McCartney stable, 'Please Please Me'.

And this is where the Beatle legend really begins.

The A-side was a superbly integrated arrangement of artful guitar, trusty harmonica and absolutely devastating block harmonies which owed more than a passing nod to the Everly Brothers' 'Cathy's Clown' – the whole up-tempo structure being decorated by crisp drum-breaks and matchless timing. If the first ten seconds of a record sell a song (as Tin Pan Alley pundits used to affirm) then 'Please Please Me' fulfilled this condition in style. The vitality of the music was complemented by the sexual leer inherent in the lyric: takes two to heavy-pet, sang John.

'Please Please Me' was the prototype for the next five years of British music. It shot virtually unhindered to the top slot, and (save for 'Penny Lane') was the first of an unbroken chain of chart-toppers which lasted through until May 1969. The B-side, 'Ask Me Why', somewhat in the tradition of the earlier flipside, 'P.S. I Love You', simultaneously established the Beatle romantic tradition that was to coalesce with 'This Boy' (B-side of 'I Want To Hold Your Hand') and reach fruition on the superb 'Hard Day's Night' album some eighteen months later.

'From Me To You' (John and Paul)/'Thank You Girl' (John and Paul)
Parlophone R 5015. Produced: George Martin
Released: April 11, 1963

In retrospect, it seems as if the Beatles, thunderstruck by the success of their previous single, played safe with this, their third outing. Certainly it owes more to the singalong qualities of 'Love Me Do' than to the musical ground-breaking of 'Please Please Me'. The song was immediately accessible, and the professional tricks (such as the importance of a strong 'hook', recently learned) were well to the fore. But the instrumentation was far more powerfully recorded, and the song's instant appeal is undeniable. Certainly foreign artists, quickly catching on to the Beatles' appeal, found 'From Me To You' far easier to cover than the difficult and idiosyncratic 'Please Please Me'.

It's interesting to note that this track, unlike their first two singles, didn't find its way onto their début album: the somewhat mediocre B-side emphasises – again in retrospect – that this was a holding operation . . . while the Beatles girded their loins for the major assault on world record markets that was to follow.

PLEASE PLEASE ME
Parlophone PCS 3042. Produced: George Martin
Released: April 1963
I Saw Her Standing There (Paul)/Misery (John and Paul)/Anna (John)/Chains (George)/ Boys (Ringo)/Ask Me Why (John)/Please Please Me (John)/Love Me Do (Paul)/P.S. I Love You (Paul)/Baby It's You (John)/Do You Want To Know a Secret? (George)/A Taste Of Honey (Paul)/There's a Place (John and Paul)/Twist and Shout (John)

As the story goes, it took sixteen hours to record the Beatles' first album. By contemporary standards, it was slightly ragged at the edges – but this was due to freshness, enthusiasm, and the undeniable fact that EMI were not, at that stage, prepared to spend money in excess

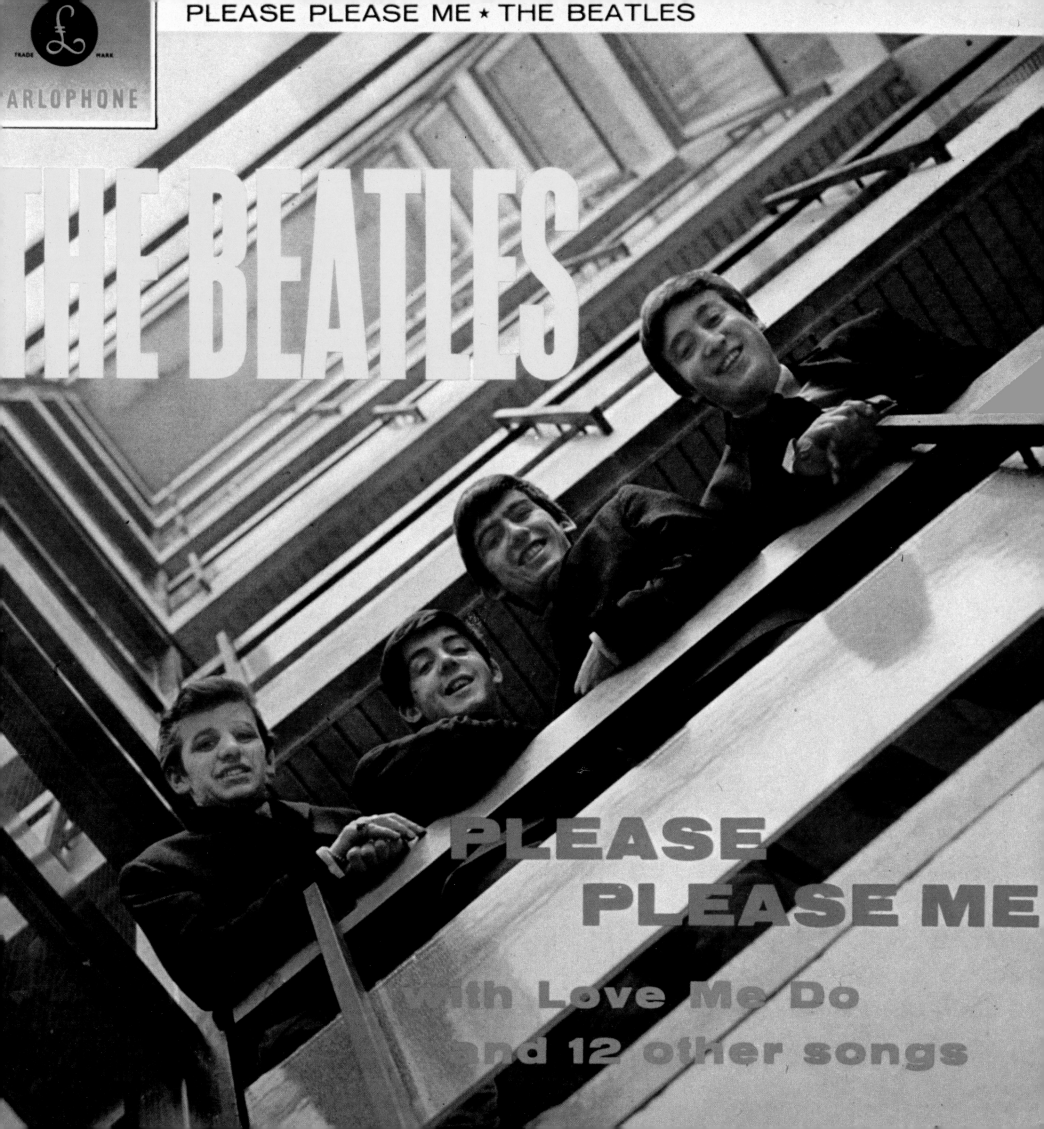

August 3
Beatles make their 294th (and final) appearance at the Cavern.

October 13
'Sunday Night at the London Palladium' brings the hysteria into the front rooms of a million homes.

November 4
Royal Command Performance: the House of Windsor rattles its jewellery.

'On the next number, would those in the cheap seats clap their hands? The rest of you rattle your jewellery.'
John Lennon on stage at the Royal Variety Command Performance.

THE BEATLES BY ROYAL COMMAND

Reporter: *'Do you have a leading lady for your first film?'*
George: *'We're trying to get the Queen. She sells.'*

of their 'normal' studio budget.

They really got their money's worth.

The album reflected the Beatles' stage act at the time, being composed of originals plus the tested rockers (from New York's Brill Building song-factory, then world centre for pop song writing). The opening track, 'I Saw Her Standing There' (later covered by Tony Newley), remains one of the great rock classics of all time, and became the third all-British example (the first two being Cliff Richard's 'Move It' and Johnny Kidd's 'Shakin' All Over'). Unlike some of the other tracks, 'I Saw Her Standing There' could have been recorded by the Beatles – or any other band – at any time in their career and would have received the same acclaim. It's timeless. The second Lennon/McCartney original, 'Misery', was a catchy, adenoidal harmony job (between John and Paul) which indicated the composing direction they'd been following some two years before (note the resemblance in style to 'From Me To You' and 'Love Me Do', also vintage self-compositions).

'Do You Want To Know a Secret?' was given to George as a solo outing (and later provided a hit for Billy J. Kramer, another NEMS artist). Kramer, in fact, made a better job of it than Harrison, whose pitching was slightly awry, and whose falsetto cracked under the strain in several places. The power was turned on again for the last of the new Lennon/McCartney originals, 'There's a Place', a superb piece of close-harmony work that followed the 'Please Please Me' harmonic tradition.

The non-originals, as already stated, were taken largely from the Beatles' then stage-act repertoire, itself derived from material written originally for black East Coast girl groups, such as the Shirelles and the Cookies – with a separate track, 'Anna', by John's beloved Arthur Alexander. (Another Alexander track, perhaps his best, 'A Shot Of Rhythm and Blues', was never to be recorded by the Beatles for official issue, though they featured it on stage in their Hamburg days.) The Cookies' 'Chains' – written by Brill songwriters Goffin and King – fitted their style as if it had been conceived with them in mind. Perhaps the archetypal bop-bop-shoo-wop tune of all time, the Shirelles' 'Boys' was given to Ringo (a canny move). And 'Baby It's You', again originally recorded by the Shirelles, was handled by Lennon with superb sensuality and sensitivity.

'The Beatles are good, clean and enjoyable entertainment and the young people like them. There is nothing we can do about it. Unnecessary and superior criticism won't do any good, but merely strengthen the usual argument: "you don't understand".'
Rev Michael Brierly of Dines Green.

1963

1963

And the World was pleased too. (From New Musical Express.)

You've PLEASED PLEASED us !

Thank You, Folks

**Paul
John
George
Ringo**

'I get my spasms of being intellectual. I read about politics but I don't think I'd vote for anyone: no messages from any phoney politicians are coming through me.' John Lennon.

'The Mersey Sound is the voice of 80,000 crumbling houses and 30,000 people on the dole.' 'The Daily Worker'.

Paul McCartney's predilection for cabaret-style songs (he'd wanted to record 'Besame Mucho') surfaced in 'A Taste Of Honey' – which also featured The Beatles' earliest concessions to the contemporary fad of double-tracking; happily, it worked – and the imaginative creak into 4/4 time for the middle eight was a masterstroke.

At the end of the session, while the Beatles were consuming tea, producer George Martin came into the studio and proclaimed: 'Boys, we need one more to make up the quota.' A swift discussion followed and the Beatles promptly returned to the mikes to perform (in one take, so legend has it) an old warhorse, the Isley Brothers' 'Twist and Shout'. This is probably the most significant track on the entire album: it provided a cataclysmic clincher to Beatles' stage shows; it yielded a best-selling EP (which climbed to Number Two in the *singles* chart); and the six-bar orgasmic ascendant – surely the highest point ever reached in any pop song – provided a forerunner for all football stadium triumphal chants. The Beatles found themselves unable to dispense with 'Twist and Shout' for at least two years as a result.

'She Loves You' (John and Paul)/'I'll Get You' (John and Paul)
Parlophone R 5055. Produced: George Martin
Released: August 23, 1963

If a future archivist were to select one single tune to characterise the Beatles' appeal and the stylistic devices for which they became world famous, he would be forced to choose 'She Loves You'.

Apart from any other musical considerations, the 'hook' – the famous 'Yeah, yeah, yeah' chorus – is so instantly appealing, even eleven years later, that the phenomenal success of this song (and of the Beatles themselves on the strength of it) is easy to understand. From the opening two bars of drums the sheer power is compelling – perhaps the incessant 'yeah's' were that kind of delightful irritant factor?

'The Beatles' Hits'
Parlophone GEP 8880. Produced: George Martin
Released: September 1963
From Me To You/Thank You Girl/Please Please Me/Love Me Do

Three of the titles on this first Beatles extended player had already scored heavily as hits in their own right. An interesting quote from the sleeve notes (by then Beatles publicist Tony Barrow) runs as follows:

'The four numbers on this EP have been selected from the Lennon & McCartney Songbook. If that description sounds a trifle pompous perhaps I may suggest you preserve this sleeve for ten years, exhume it from your collection somewhere around the middle of 1973 and write me a very nasty letter if the pop people of the 70s aren't talking with respect about at least two of these titles as "Early examples of modern Beat standards taken from the Lennon & McCartney Songbook".'

'Twist and Shout'
Parlophone GEP 8882. Produced: George Martin
Released: September 1963
Twist and Shout/A Taste Of Honey/Do You Want To Know a Secret?/There's a Place

The rush-release of this EP – the second within one month – containing tracks from the best-selling 'Please Please Me' LP showed that, finally, EMI Records were catching on to the potential represented by the Beatles. Their assessment of the size of the Beatles' market proved fairly shrewd: this EP rocketed to the Number Two placing in the *singles* chart – in the face of determined opposition from Brian Poole's 'Twist and Shout' single (the last time an artist was to provoke a direct confrontation with the Beatles).

A television performance. Note the absence of guitar leads!

'I Want To Hold Your Hand' (John and Paul)/'This Boy' (John and Paul)
Parlophone: R 5084. Produced: George Martin
Released: November 29, 1963

With the release of this superb and historic single, the Beatles proved themselves masters of the difficult art of writing original, memorable and commercial pop singles. The musical structure of 'I Want To Hold Your Hand' is full of subtle tricks and adventurous ploys that reveal a rapidly growing maturity in their work. From the deliberate stumble of the opening time-signature to the calculated dissonances of the chorus, the whole conception of this song was unlike anything attempted before – and owed little or nothing to their well-publicised tap-root American influences.

America, until now a sealed market for British rock acts (including the Beatles' own earlier material – but that's another story), sagged to its alpaca knees in awe. Thus is history made.

The status of the B-side, hitherto a reluctant chore performed to prevent the embarrassment of one-sided records (this very idea had actually been under consideration by the industry), was refurbished by the inclusion of the Beatles' classiest flip to date, the truly magnificent

'I don't feel like I imagine an idol is supposed to feel.' Paul McCartney.

'For heaven's sake don't say we're the new youth, because that's a load of rubbish.' Paul McCartney.

'The Police in each town are competing against one another to see who can get the Beatles out of the theatre the quickest.' A reporter.

21

1963

Below *The ad men were not slow to jump on to the bandwagon.*

Below right *The Liverpool lads express their opinions on 'Juke Box Jury'.*

Opposite page *A trend-setting sleeve for the second album. This device was subsequently much plagiarised.*

'This Boy', a three-part choral romance job that again pointed the way towards 'A Hard Day's Night' with its high-quality balladry. In particular, listen for the movement in Paul's unstrained top line and the shift from tonic to sub-mediant in Lennon's (lower) vocal.

'The Beatles No. 1'
Parlophone GEP 8883. Produced: George Martin
Released: November 1963
I Saw Her Standing There/Misery/Anna/Chains

Old Ukrainian proverb: why release a Beatles record once when you can release it twice (or even three times)? EMI, catching on fast by this time, presented the public with further lucrative skimmings from . . . you guessed it, the 'Please Please Me' album.

WITH THE BEATLES
Parlophone PCS 3045. Produced: George Martin
Released: November 22, 1963
It Won't Be Long (John)/All I've Got To Do (John)/All My Loving (Paul)/Don't Bother Me (George)/Little Child (John)/Till There Was You (Paul)/Please Mr Postman (John)/Roll Over Beethoven (George)/Hold Me Tight (Paul)/You Really Got a Hold On Me (John)/I Want To Be Your Man (Ringo)/Devil In Her Heart (George)/Not a Second Time (John)/Money (John)

This is the only LP from the primitive early 'sixties that, well over ten years later, still retains all the freshness and breadth of musical vision that was instantly apparent on the day of issue. It was a simply staggering achievement from every point of view, a landmark *par excellence*, and one of the four best albums the Beatles ever made. Even the cover design was a radical departure from the accepted style. Production quality was up, the overall standard of the music was higher – and even EMI's budget was a considerable advance on the earlier sessions, which must prove something.

Faith in the Beatles as composers – and in George Martin as a producer – was shown by the inclusion of no less than eight hitherto unreleased Beatles originals (including George Harrison's first recorded composition, 'Don't Bother Me'). And, highly significantly, there was no need to hang the album on the chart success of a previous single.

PAUL McCARTNEY   RINGO STARR   GEORGE

**with
the
beatles**

stereo **1963**

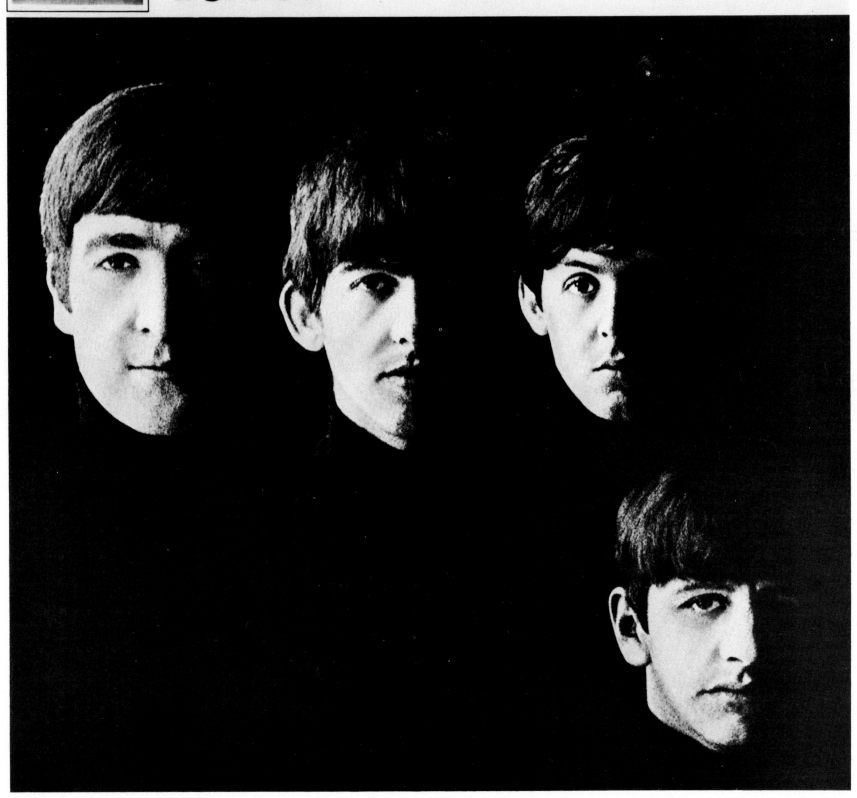

1963

"The smartest men in Spain gave LYBRO the 'Flamenco' idea!"

SAYS **GEORGE HARRISON.**

(Lead guitar and vocalist)

Is the Flamenco dancer the smartest man in Europe? Could be! And LYBRO have captured all his clean-limbed, masculine elegance in this sensational jean.

Deep waistband with back lacing; splayed ankle cuffs; white stitching and trim.

Opposite page and above *From* New Musical Express, *1963.*
Below *Such souvenirs were to become common in the Beatlemania years.*

Track by track: 'It Won't Be Long', which perhaps owed something in inspiration to 'From Me To You', was far superior to the early tune in its vitality, musical subtlety (note the use of the flattened sub-mediant in the last bars of the chorus) and in the strength of the vocal. This, and the second track 'All I've Got To Do', best sum up the album's musical direction. The latter is an extraordinary piece of song writing by Lennon, indicating his continued Arthur Alexander influences.

'All My Loving', sung by Paul with super-fast guitar triplets from Lennon in the background and a superb guitar solo from George (certainly his best instrumental work to date), was concrete proof that the Beatles' standard of composition was such that they were able to include, as album tracks, material that lesser artists would have been delighted to accept as singles (demand for this one track was so heavy that, three months later, it was issued as the prime track on an EP). George Harrison's 'Don't Bother Me' came next: his curious nasal monotone, backed by imaginative guitar work, figured strongly on what was perhaps one of his best-ever compositions.

'Little Child', a fast raucous duet between John and Paul, lay firmly along another of their established style-lines: the 'catchy singalong'. 'Till There Was You' featured McCartney-as-Copacabana-balladeer; the BBC loved it, and so did guitarists, especially for the lustrous duet work between John and George – in particular the magnificent melodic solo from Harrison which echoed Charlie Byrd's work.

As usual with the Beatles, the best track is the last. 'Please Mr Postman' (one of three Motown numbers included on this album) showed an under-emphasised aspect of the Beatles as musicians: they could, almost without exception, cover other peoples' material and make it sound convincing. 'Postman', with Lennon in strong voice, lent itself to their personalised style of harmony-with-high-spirits. Excellent deployment of the three voices and power to spare.

Side Two, and Chuck Berry's classic 'Roll Over Beethoven' (hitherto sung by Lennon on stage but handed to Harrison to boost his vocal contribution). It later became a massive individual hit for the Beatles in America. The poorest track, 'Hold Me Tight', fails because McCartney's vision of the completed tune obviously sagged somewhat, and his distressingly out-of-tune singing became quite embarrassing after only a few bars.

Smokey Robinson's 'You Really Got a Hold On Me' is such a stern test for any vocalist that it takes utter self-confidence even to attempt it: Lennon, renowned for such virtues, did so and came through with a stunning version that, if less than the original, is only so because Lennon was over-respectful. The obligatory Ringo track, 'I Wanna Be Your Man', pounds along in great style (it simultaneously became the first major hit for the Rolling Stones).

Harrison surfaced again on 'Devil In Her Heart'; Lennon delivers the final Beatle original, 'Not a Second Time', in fairly unmemorable style and the set closes with Barrett Strong's classic 'Money', one of the most-covered rock tunes of all time (and later re-recorded by Lennon with the Plastic Ono Band on the 'Live Peace in Toronto' LP).

'I'd like to end up sort of unforgettable.' Ringo Starr.

Reporter: *'How long do you think the Beatles will last?'*
John: *'About five years.'*

'Don't let the Beatles come here.' Miss Mary McNamee, Deputy Mayoress of Blackburn.

Reporter: *'Why do you wear all those rings on your fingers?'*
Ringo: *'Because I can't get them through my nose.'*

December 21/January 11 'The Beatles Christmas Show' – scintillating songs and racy repartee – plus a cast of thousands.

Life-lines of the BEATLES

	JOHN	**PAUL**	**GEORGE**	**RINGO** (STARR)
Real name :	John Lennon	Paul McCartney	George Harrison	Richard Starkey
Birth date :	October 9, 1940.	June 18, 1942.	February 25, 1942.	July, 7, 1940.
Birthplace :	Liverpool.	Liverpool.	Liverpool.	Liverpool.
Height :	5 ft. 11 in.	5 ft. 11 in.	5 ft. 11 in.	5 ft. 8 in.
Weight :	11 st. 5 lb.	11 st. 4 lb.	10 st. 2 lb.	9 st. 8 lb.
Colour of eyes :	Brown.	Hazel.	Dark brown.	Blue.
Colour of hair :	Brown.	Black.	Brown.	Dark brown.
Brothers, sisters :	None.	Mike.	Louise, Peter and Harry.	None.
Instruments played :	Rhythm guitar, harmonica, percussion, piano.	Bass guitar, drums, piano, banjo.	Guitar, piano, drums.	Drums, guitar.
Educated :	Quarry Bank Grammar and Liverpool College of Art.	Liverpool Institute High School.	Liverpool Institute High School.	Liverpool Secondary Modern, Riversdale Technical College.
Age entered show business :	20.	18.	17.	18.
Former occupation:	Art student.	Student.	Student.	Engineer.
Hobbies :	Writing songs, poems and plays; girls, painting, TV, meeting people.	Girls, songwriting, sleeping.	Driving, records, girls.	Night-driving, sleeping, Westerns.
Favourite singers :	Shirelles, Miracles, Chuck Jackson, Ben E. King.	Ben E. King, Little Richard, Chuck Jackson, Larry Williams.	Little Richard, Eartha Kitt.	Brook Benton, Sam "Lightning" Hopkins.
Favourite actors :	Robert Mitchum, Peter Sellers.	Marlon Brando, Tony Perkins.	Vic Morrow.	Paul Newman, Jack Palance.
Favourite actresses:	Juliette Greco, Sophia Loren.	Brigitte Bardot, Juliette Greco.	Brigitte Bardot.	Brigitte Bardot.
Favourite foods :	Curry and jelly.	Chicken Maryland.	Lamb chops, chips.	Steak.
Favourite drinks :	Whisky and tea.	Milk.	Tea.	Whisky.
Favourite clothes :	Sombre.	Good suits, suede.	Anything.	Suits.
Favourite band :	Quincy Jones.	Billy Cotton.	Duane Eddy group.	Arthur Lyman.
Favourite instrumentalist :	Sonny Terry.	None special.	Chet Atkins.	None special.
Favourite composers :	Luther Dixon.	Goffin-King.	None special.	Bert Bacharach McCartney and Lennon.
Likes :	Blondes, leather.	Music, TV.	Driving.	Fast cars.
Dislikes :	Stupid people.	Shaving.	Haircuts.	Onions and Donald Duck.
Tastes in music :	R-and-b, gospel.	R-and-b, modern jazz.	Spanish guitar, c-and-w.	C-and-w, r-and-b.
Personal ambitions :	To write musical.	To have my picture in the " Dandy."	To design a guitar.	To be happy.
Professional ambition :	To be rich and famous.	To popularise our sound.	To fulfil all group's hopes.	To get to the top.

1964

January
Beatlemania not yet visible in Paris as Beatles sweat it out trying to impress unimpressionable L'Olympia audience intent on singing along with Trini Lopez and watching Sylvie Vartan pout 'n' pose. Les Français? Pfui!

February 7
Nervous Beatles land at Kennedy Airport, New York, to meticulously well-planned mass welcome — first of the airport hysteria scenes. Ringo saves duff Ed Sullivan TV Show and the Beatles play Carnegie Hall.

March
Commence frolicking about before movie cameras for *A Hard Day's Night*.

Below *The Beatles hit L'Olympia, Paris, but the French were more interested in Sylvie Vartan (centre).*

Below right *Recording 'Can't Buy Me Love'.*

'**All My Loving**'
Parlophone GEP 8891. Produced: George Martin
Released: February 7, 1964
All My Loving/Ask Me Why/Money/P.S. I Love You

Possibly a more imaginative course of action would have been to issue 'All My Loving' backed with 'It Won't Be Long' as an interim single. Instead, EMI marketing men referred back to that old Ukrainian proverb and issued this patchwork EP, on which 'Ask Me Why' and 'P.S. I Love You' made their third appearances within eighteen months.

'**Can't Buy Me Love**' (Paul)/'**You Can't Do That**' (John)
Parlophone R 5114. Produced: George Martin
Released: March 20, 1964

These paired tracks were the hardest, most uncompromising slabs of rock that the Beatles had so far issued in single form. Oddly enough, this was also the time when established international jazz and supper-club acts, such as Ella Fitzgerald and Count Basie, had begun to take notice of the group's success: their cover versions of Beatles' material soon elevated our heroes from mere pop phenomena to (almost) equal status with modern composers – no mean accomplishment.

Incidentally, the record inaugurated a system where the predominant writer would sing lead vocal on his own composition. The A-side featured a superbly sloppy guitar solo from George; John, a rawer guitarist altogether, switched roles with George for the flip, making *his* recorded début on lead guitar. Panache carried the day.

'Long Tall Sally'
Parlophone GEP 8913. Produced: George Martin
Released: June 19, 1964
I Call Your Name (John)/Slow Down (John and Paul)/Long Tall Sally (Paul)
/Matchbox (Ringo)

Hamburg revisited: and it must be said that McCartney's vocal (plus Harrison's breath-taking solo) on the title track absolutely shreds the original (by Little Richard) to fragments. It is doubtful if the Beatles have ever surpassed it in terms of old-fashioned high-energy rock 'n' roll.

Larry Williams' 'Slow Down' and Carl Perkins' 'Matchbox' were old on-stage chestnuts from the Star Club marathons. With a newly awakened eye on that goldmine known as composer royalties, they added 'I Call Your Name' (a mammoth hit for stablemate Billy J. Kramer). Without question, a great EP of our time and the best of these hybrid issues that the Beatles were ever to produce.

It is known that, at this point in the Beatles' career, a large selection of American rock standards were put down on tape in line with the policy of storing future material in the eventuality of a break-up or a regrettable indisposition. Contrary to the claims on the sleeve notes of published albums and EPs, the Beatles did *not* have enough songs to 'keep them busy for the next ten years'. Hence the precaution.

1964

March 23
John Lennon's first book *In His Own Write* wins prestigious Foyle's Literary Prize. As guest speaker at celebratory banquet, Lennon mumbles and flees.

'Thank you very much. You've got a lucky face.' John Lennon's entire acceptance speech at Foyle's celebrated Literary Luncheon held in his honour.

Reporter: *'What do you call that hair style?'*
George: *'Arthur!'*

'The Beatles — they're a passing phase: symptoms of the uncertainty of the times and the confusion about us.' Dr Billy Graham.

Above *New York, and here they are rehearsing with Ed Sullivan (centre) for his nationwide TV show.*

Above right *Illustrations from Lennon's In His Own Write.*

Right *America has discovered the Beatles — in no uncertain terms.*

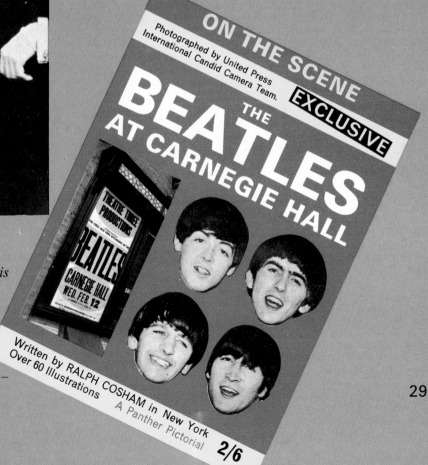

March 31
United States 'Billboard' Chart:
(1) 'Can't Buy Me Love', (2) 'Twist and Shout', (3) 'She Loves You', (4) 'I Want To Hold Your Hand' and (5) 'Please Please Me' – plus Nos. 16, 44, 49, 69, 78, 84 and 88 in the same Hot Hundred.

May 6
'Around the Beatles' TV show.

May/June
Ringo hospitalised with tonsilitis for Danish, Dutch and Far-Eastern jaunt. Drummer Jimmy Nicol fills the vacant chair, enjoys fifteen minutes of instant fame . . . and is never heard of again.

Above *Paul with drummer Jimmy Nicol at Amsterdam.*

Opposite page *Sleeve for 'A Hard Day's Night'.*

'A Hard Day's Night' (John plus Paul)/'Things We Said Today' (Paul)
Parlophone R 5160. Produced: George Martin
Released: July 1964

The Beatles branch out. All previous compositions had been governed by the merits of the song in question. This, however, was a movie theme – a premeditated piece of song writing brought about by the needs of making their first (and best) movie.

This single, plus the immaculate album of the same name, strongly features George Harrison on twelve-string Rickenbacker guitar (his opening chord is Gm7 add 11 – for those who collect such information).

'Things We Said Today', one of McCartney's most distinctive early compositions, is almost entirely constructed around two chords, and is therefore typical of much of their material from this period.

George Martin emerges – for perhaps the first time – as not only a producer, but an arranger *and* a contributing instrumentalist (it's his piano you hear doubling the guitar solo line on 'A Hard Day's Night').

A HARD DAY'S NIGHT
Parlophone PCS 3058. Produced: George Martin
Released: July 10, 1964
A Hard Day's Night (John plus Paul)/I Should Have Known Better (John)/If I Fell (John and Paul)/I'm Happy Just To Dance With You (George)/And I Love Her (Paul)/Tell Me Why (John, Paul and George)/Can't Buy Me Love (Paul)/Any Time At All (John)/I'll Cry Instead (John)/Things We Said Today (Paul)/When I Get Home (John)/You Can't Do That (John)/I'll Be Back (John and Paul)

The challenge of making a motion picture caught the Beatles on a strong upswing following the unprecedented success of the months beforehand; the result was incomparably their finest work so far. 'A Hard Day's Night', both filmed and recorded versions, not only struck Beatlemania paydirt, it *is* Beatlemania itself – captured in exactly the way in which most people fantasised it.

The music? Correspondingly innocent. Among the top echelon of total Beatle product, 'A Hard Day's Night' is still by far the most overtly romantic. It is even naive. Yet, unlike similar music by lesser artists, it utterly failed to embarrass: the effect is wholly positive.

'I Should Have Known Better' is almost an extension of the title track, retaining the key of G major, the same tempo and the same overall feel. And, like most of the tracks on this album, it is strongly influenced by George Harrison's newly acquired twelve-string Rickenbacker guitar – a revolutionary instrument for 1964, (which, in turn, was to influence to the strongest degree the then-embryonic American West-Coast rock scene – via Roger 'Jim' McGuinn of the Byrds, a besotted Harrison worshipper).

'If I Fell', though sentimental, was the most appealing love song the Beatles had written to date. Lennon and McCartney (low and high harmonies respectively) caress the melody through with a degree of care that underscored the album's basic premise of excellence-through-innocence. Yet the Beatles' professional ability to compose with a definite aim in mind had not deteriorated, as was shown on 'I'm Happy Just To Dance With You'. For a Beatle song of this period, this shows definite signs of 'blueprinting' – but this small criticism doesn't detract from the track's definite qualities of danceability and commercial appeal; George – who had no compositions of his own on 'A Hard Day's Night – sang. 'Tell Me Why' bears hallmarks of the same sort. But the track in between was McCartney's finest composition to date: 'And I Love Her' illustrates his growing ability to write charming, insubstantial melodies with a high 'haunt count' (an aptitude he still retains). Like no less than three other tracks from this album it became a million-plus selling single in America: its 'standard'

1964

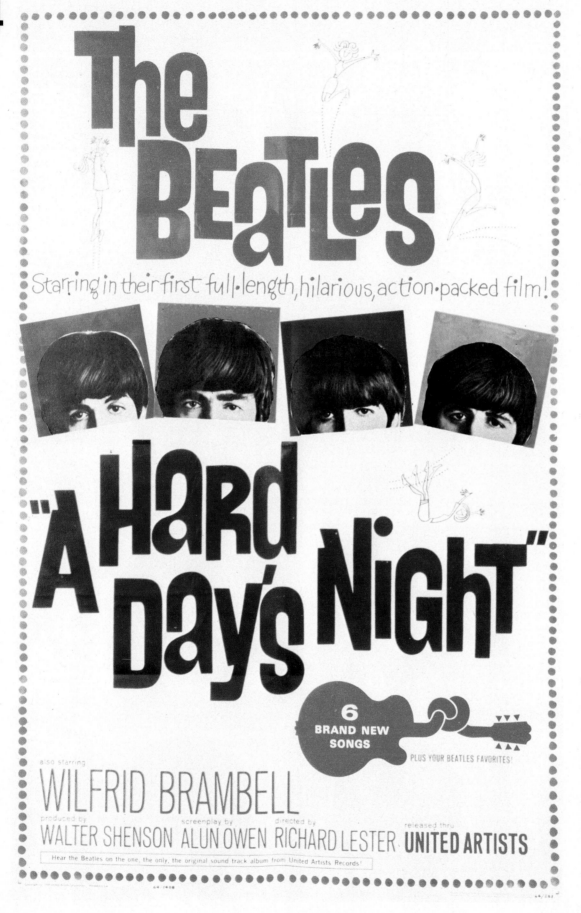

'I think they are lovely boys, and I've been dying to meet them. Harold and I are both tremendous fans of the Beatles and always listen to them and watch them on television. Harold and I met in Liverpool. Even in those days we used the word "gear", meaning fabulous or wonderful.' Mrs Harold Wilson.

These pages *Enter our heroes as film stars in* A Hard Day's Night, *directed by that master of zany, apparently ad-libbed comedies, Dick Lester. Their first film was a challenge which they met with seemingly effortless enthusiasm, and the public responded in kind. The film was also the occasion of the first meeting between George and his wife-to-be, Patti Boyd (*opposite bottom*).

potential showed when it later materialised, spread over a light beguine tempo, on the music-stands of ten thousand clip-joint dance bands – by no means the last Beatle melody to do so.

'A Hard Day's Night', as a musical entity, also set another precedent in that it was the first great on-the-road album. Rightly, the group felt that their reservoir of originals and rock chestnuts was unsuitable for such a major production. For the first time, therefore, they were compelled to compose to a very tight schedule and to a preconceived style idea. They endured their goldfish-bowl existence manfully, composing all thirteen tracks while experiencing siege conditions in Paris and New York. In the event, only seven tracks were used in the film. And two had already been previewed as singles.

The remaining six make up Side Two of 'A Hard Day's Night'. If anything, these cuts are superior. Two, at least – 'Things We Said Today' and 'I'll Be Back' – are superb illustrations of the Beatles' flowering ability to create strong melodies. 'I'll Cry Instead' is a precursor of a country beat the group were to explore more fully on their next album. 'Any Time At All' and 'When I Get Home', both Lennon's songs, herald a forthcoming crack in the romantic façade which basically characterises the album.

'I'll Cry Instead' became the second smash US single to be culled from this remarkable collection – and the same set was to furnish two best-selling British EPs. And 'A Hard Day's Night' was the first album to feature an exclusive repertoire of Lennon/McCartney material.

And the World said: these guys are the best song writers since Schubert.

33

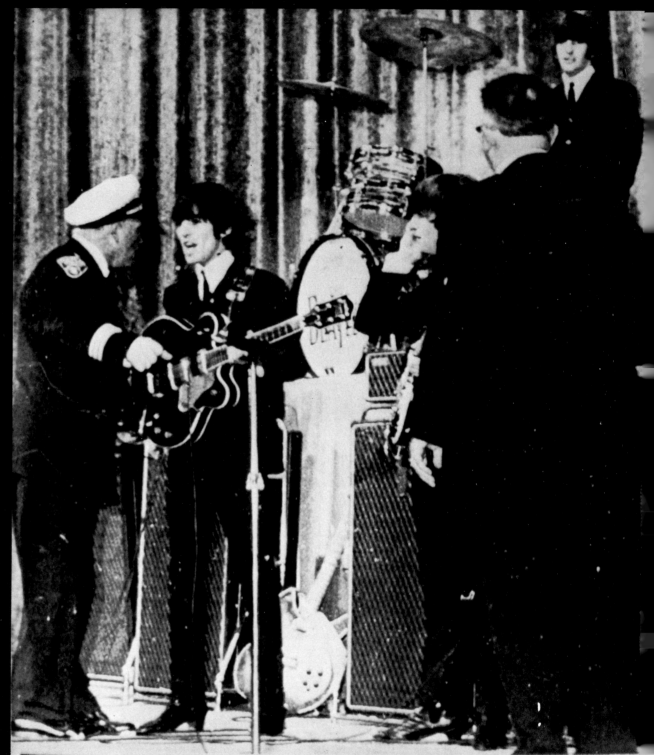

These pages *Beatlemania was at its height,
and its side-products – fan-club magazines,
badges, souvenirs, signed photographs –
were on sale almost throughout the world.
They are now valuable collectors' items.*

(CD3x)CLEVELAND,OHIO,Sept.16-(AP)-Police Inspector
Carl Bear left,of Cleveland's Juvenile Bureau,orders
Beatle George Harrison off the stage of Public Hall
Tuesday night as teenage fans rushed the stage. Bear
let the British singing group go on after the wailing
youngsters were given 15 minutes to cool off somewhat.
Man at right isn't identified.(APWirephoto)(jtm40515
gmt)1964   www

July 6
Piccadilly Circus closed to traffic for royal première of *A Hard Day's Night*.

August/September
Back in the USA for five weeks of touring.

'DISREGARD PRESS REPORTS QUOTING THE DUKE OF EDINBURGH AS SAYING BEATLES ON THE WANE SHOULD READ I THINK BEATLES ARE AWAY AT THE MOMENT MISTAKE PROBABLY DUE TO MISPRINT PRINCE PHILIP SENDS HIS BEST WISHES FOR CONTINUED SUCCESS SIGNED SQUADRON LEADER CHECKETTS'.

'Did you see that woman cut off a piece of my hair? I'm ruddy mad. This lot are terrifying – much worse than the kids.' Ringo Starr at Lord and Lady Ormsby-Gore's British Embassy Ball in Washington.

'I Feel Fine' (John)/'She's a Woman' (Paul)
Parlophone R 5200. Produced: George Martin
Released: November 27, 1964

Just about the first constructive use of guitar feedback as we know and love her today. An excruciatingly difficult riff from Harrison sustains the song throughout, the timing is peerless, and the double-lead guitar solo ahead of its time by at least three summers. Reports at the time claimed the electric shaver sound which fortuitously opens the song had been produced 'by accident' – there are those who know better.

McCartney's 'She's a Woman', the B-side of this single, shows already that he had discovered – like Lennon before him – that it was well within his capacity to write and sing original rockers of considerable power.

'A Hard Day's Night' No. 1
Parlophone GEP 8920. Produced: George Martin
Released: November 4, 1964
I Should Have Known Better/If I Fell/Tell Me Why/And I Love Her

'A Hard Day's Night No. 2'
Parlophone GEP 8924. Produced: George Martin
Released: November 6, 1964
Any Time At All/I'll Cry Instead/Things We Said Today/When I Get Home

And don't forget those two US hits.

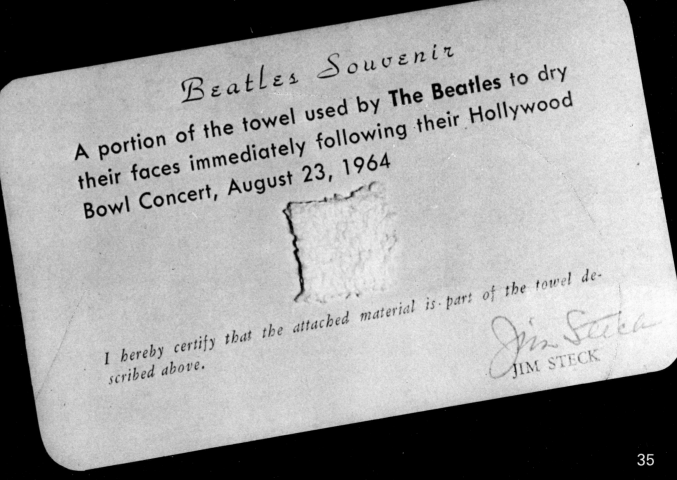

1964

BEATLES FOR SALE
Parlophone PCS 3062. Produced: George Martin
Released: November 27, 1964
No Reply (John)/I'm a Loser (John)/Baby's In Black (John and Paul)/Rock and Roll Music (John)/I'll Follow the Sun (Paul)/Mr Moonlight (John)/Kansas City (Paul)/Eight Days a Week (John and Paul)/Words Of Love (John and Paul)/Honey Don't (Ringo)/Every Little Thing (John and Paul)/I Don't Want To Spoil the Party (John)/What You're Doing (Paul)/Everybody's Trying To Be My Baby (George)

The laws of supply and demand overtook the Beatles as they reached the plateau of Beatlemania. Ideally, a longish creative rest would have suited their purposes better, but pressure was intense and a new collection had to be assembled.

It is for these reasons that 'Beatles For Sale' represented a certain tapering-off of enthusiasm – recalled, perhaps, in a sardonic and not altogether ambiguous album title. The sleeve itself was an ambitious gate-fold project (but the faces, if you look, are already betraying some weariness).

There were six non-originals: Chuck Berry's 'Rock and Roll Music', Dr Feelgood's 'Mr Moonlight', Little Richard's arrangement of 'Kansas City', Buddy Holly's 'Words Of Love', plus Carl Perkins' 'Honey Don't' and 'Everybody's Trying To Be My Baby'. All, except the last, succeed; and this represents the last major plundering of their sturdy chestnut sack.

The eight originals are all somewhat morose – especially when set in juxtaposition to the glad spirits of 'A Hard Day's Night'. The exception, perhaps, can be found in 'I'll Follow the Sun' and 'Eight Days a Week'. The former indicates a newly developing talent in McCartney – acoustic balladeer; the latter hearkens back in a curious manner to 'All My Loving' and 'No Reply'. 'I'm a Loser' and 'Baby's In Black' are downright morbid. 'Every Little Thing' and 'What You're Doing' are almost domestic gripes.

'I Don't Want To Spoil the Party' best encapsulates the country feel which is strongly apparent throughout both sides. Ringo's song (for this album) was 'Honey Don't', and George (again without a tune of his own to sing) chose Carl Perkins' 'Everybody's Trying To Be My Baby'. Note: the Beatles covered three Perkins compositions in total – first, of course, being 'Matchbox' on an earlier EP.

October/November
Scenes of mayhem accompany British tour with Mary Wells.

December/January
'Another Beatles Christmas Show'. This time, cast of thousands includes Yardbirds and Freddie and the Dreamers.

Above *Publicity for the British tour with Mary Wells.*

Right *Beatle 'official' fan badge.*

Opposite page *'Beatles for Sale' – a fine sleeve, but do those faces look slightly tired?*

'There is something magical and sinister about repetitive siblings. Mythology is very strong on them. The Beatles inspire terror, awe and reverence. I had no idea they looked so similar – just marginal differentiations on an identical theme. And with that hair they reminded me of the Midwich Cuckoos.' Jonathan Miller.

'75 per cent publicity, 20 per cent haircut and 5 per cent lilting lament.' 'New York Herald Tribune'.

1965

February 11
'I, Richard Starkey take thee
Maureen Cox to be my lawful
wedded wife.'
February/March
Recording *Help!* soundtrack, in
between running around in circles:
London, the Bahamas and Austria.

April 11
Collect more silverware at *New
Musical Express* Pollwinners'
Concert.

'A Ticket To Ride' (John)/'Yes It Is' (John and Paul)
Parlophone R 5265. Produced: George Martin
Released: April 9, 1965

The boom in British music which the Beatles themselves had stimulated had, by the beginning of 1965, resolved itself into intense competition between many other promising bands. The Merseybeat boom eventually degenerated into a vague, showbizzy, commercial series of faceless entities but, from the London-based rhythm 'n blues boom, many excellent instrumentalists had already materialised: Eric Clapton, Pete Townshend, Keith Richard and Jeff Beck. The Beatles now found themselves having to compete on a wholly different level. It is to their credit that they did so.

'Ticket To Ride' was unquestionably their most ambitious piece of musical structuring to date: all the playing displayed is of the high standard necessary for the group to retain their credibility among the previously-mentioned *coterie* of new, talented instrumentalists. Perhaps most to the fore was Ringo, who proved that he wasn't just a 'Lovable Nose' by drumming skilfully (including massively-accented triplets) on this, the first of the mid-period Beatle singles.

Pungent lyrics add strength to the tune, which also features Paul McCartney on lead guitar (he plays the solos at the end of each middle eight). The weightiness of the piece was accentuated by the harshness of the lyrics – which reveal Lennon as a misogynistic cynic – a role he was later to have much trouble in abandoning.

'Yes It Is' furthered the Beatles' instrumental credentials – although it wasn't too original (for them), being a remake of 'This Boy'; it strongly featured a new rock 'n roll device, the volume/tone pedal, played by George Harrison. This track is fairly innocuous but rather forgettable and doesn't match the power or the fieriness of the A-side.

An interesting anecdote about 'Ticket To Ride' centres around US Capitol Records and their by now insatiable hunger for Beatle product. Jumping the gun somewhat, they issued the single as being 'From the film "Eight Arms To Hold You"' (the provisional title for the Beatles' second movie; it was, of course, later re-titled *Help!*).

Ringo weds Maureen Cox, February 11.
The others are, left to right: Mr Cox,

Cynthia Lennon, Mrs Cox, John, George,
Brian Epstein, Mr Starkey and Mrs Starkey.

1965

June 12
It is announced that the four Liverpool lads have been awarded gongs (MBEs) for 'services to export'. Irate colonels and ex-RAF heroes deluge Buckingham Palace with returned ornamental metal and ribbons.

'I didn't think you got an MBE for playing rock 'n' roll.' George Harrison.

'Being awarded the MBE – I can't believe it. I thought you had to drive tanks and win wars.' John Lennon.

'There's a proper medal, isn't there? I'll keep it to wear when I'm old.' Ringo Starr.

These pages *1965, and the Beatles are making their second film,* Help!*. They have also just been awarded the* MBE. *The black-and-white photograph above shows Ringo's and Paul's reaction to the news during a press interview at the film studios; the others are stills from the film itself.*

'Beatles For Sale No. 1'
Parlophone GEP 8931. Produced: George Martin
Released: April 6, 1965
No Reply/I'm a Loser/Rock and Roll Music/Eight Days a Week

'Beatles For Sale No. 2'
Parlophone GEP 8938. Produced: George Martin
Released: June 4, 1965
I'll Follow the Sun/Baby's In Black/Words Of Love/I Don't Want To Spoil the Party

Old Ukrainian saying: if it moves, sell it.

'Help!' (John)/'I'm Down' (Paul)
Parlophone R 5305. Produced: George Martin
Released: July 23, 1965

The Beatles were becoming masters at supplying what was needed *when* it was needed. All the same, 'Help!' lacked a little motivation and direction. The lyrics are certainly better than the tune; this leads the listener to suspect that, for Lennon at least, the gilt was beginning to wear off the gingerbread (he later avowed complete distaste towards the movie *Help!*, for which this song was written).

Yet it features still another superb throwaway guitar line from George Harrison's Gretsch.

The B-side was a format rocker in the Berry style; although they selected it for their set on the famous Shea Stadium concert, it lacked the punch of earlier tunes in the same mould, especially 'She's a Woman'.

1965

June 24
A Spaniard In The Works by John Lennon available from all good booksellers.

July 29
Royal première of *Help!*

HELP!
Parlophone PCS 3071. Produced: George Martin
Released: August 1965
Help! (John)/The Night Before (Paul)/You've Got To Hide Your Love Away (John)/I Need You (George)/Another Girl (Paul)/You're Gonna Lose That Girl (John)/Ticket To Ride (John)/Act Naturally (Ringo)/It's Only Love (John)/You Like Me Too Much (George)/Tell Me What You See (John and Paul)/I've Just Seen a Face (Paul)/Yesterday (Paul)/Dizzy Miss Lizzy (John)

'Help!' catches the Beatles fighting for breath but still apparently happy to go along with the charade. Like 'A Hard Day's Night', the album owes its very existence to a movie project; unlike the earlier excursion, something is definitely lacking.

There's a certain degree of (almost inevitable) cynicism, a corresponding lack of enthusiasm and a couple of looming mantraps; McCartney's predilection for schmaltz bursts into full horrendous flower on the overly-praised and much covered 'Yesterday' (which, for a couple of years, boasted a working title of 'Scrambled Eggs'). The production, sadly, is the poorest of all Beatle albums, being thin, mean and lacking in any real positive energy.

The US version was an exceptionally poor compilation of just seven soundtrack songs – the

At the première of Help! *with wives Maureen and Cynthia.*

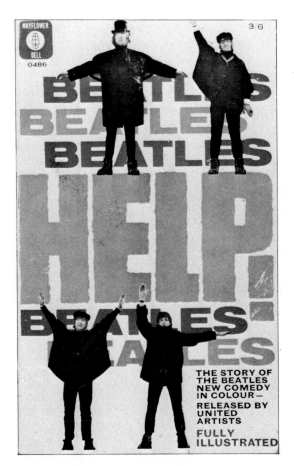

Help! *again: the book, the record sleeve, and the peaked-capped John.*

whole of side one – supported by some undistinguished George Martin muzak, overly influenced by curry-restaurant sitar and too many James Bond movies.

Few of the tracks really deserve individual comment; perhaps the best of the soundtrack originals was 'You're Going To Lose That Girl'. Lennon's escalating infatuation with Bob Dylan took the form of silly peaked caps (in the movie) and 'You've Got To Hide Your Love Away' (on the record). Ringo parodied his earlier success (as an actor) by burbling the country-flavoured 'Act Naturally' – which incidentally gave the Beatles yet another American hit single.

George, for his part, made a manful attempt to crack the commercial coconut by singing two of his own compositions; unfortunately, neither really lift this album – or his composing status – out of its built-in slough of despond. It's an indictment of 'Help!' that the best track, 'Ticket To Ride', had already scored as a single.

THE BEATLES AT

STADIUM

The great Shea Stadium concert, and our heroes make the most of the rather sparse toilet facilities. The vast size of the stadium itself is seen to its best advantage in this

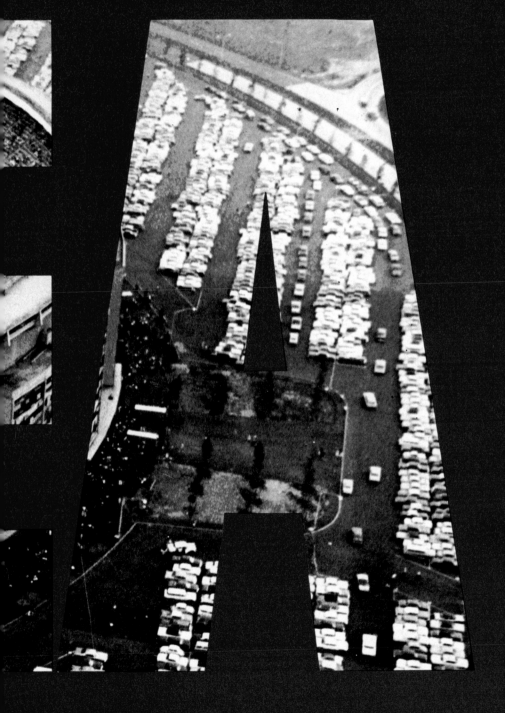

aerial view: never before in the history of musical entertainment has there been an audience to equal the numbers – 60,000 plus – that filled it on that historic night.

45

1965

August
Beatles re-conquer America for the
third time — opening with legendary
Shea Stadium concert (15
August).

'Over 55,000 people saw the Beatles
at Shea Stadium. We took 304,000
dollars, the greatest gross ever in the
history of show business.'
Promoter Sid Bernstein.

All on these pages *Behind the scenes and
on-stage at the Shea Stadium: the opposite
page (top) features Brian Epstein
anxiously watching his lads. The TV film
– utilising no less than twelve camera
crews – followed in detail the Beatles'
journey from central Manhattan to Shea, as
well as making the most of the on-stage
sequences. At every traffic intersection the
police opened up the way for the cop-
escorted convoy, while at the concert
itself 2000 security men struggled to keep
the fans in line. Quite an operation.*

RUBBER SOUL
Parlophone PCS 3075. Produced: George Martin
Released: December 3, 1965
Drive My Car (Paul)/Norwegian Wood (John)/You Won't See Me (Paul)/Nowhere Man (John)/Think For Yourself (Paul)/The Word (John and Paul)/Michelle (Paul)/What Goes On (Ringo)/Girl (John)/I'm Looking Through You (Paul)/In My Life (John)/Wait (John and Paul)/ If I Needed Someone (George)/Run For Your Life (John)

There is so much of consequence on this album that we now enter the territory where critical commentary becomes almost purely subjective. For a start, it's crushingly obvious that the brief hiatus which had lingered during the 'Beatles For Sale'/'Help!' period had been banished – perhaps with a little assistance from a certain shapely and verdant (and illegal) mid-oriental plant?

'Rubber Soul' is the Beatles' first step into the mystic and, although subsequent albums seemed to extrapolate these visions much further, the insight – and cutting social comment – showed that the group had ditched the jelly babies forever. They were a studio band pure and simple – touring had long since become a question of going through the motions.

Above *Recording 'Paperback Writer'*.

Right *Yet another trend-setting sleeve.*

1965

October
They are invested at Buckingham Palace with their MBEs. Nerves compel consumption of illicit drugs beforehand in Palace loo.

December
Short nine-day whistle-stop around Britain with Moody Blues: the last time they were to tour the Motherland.

The Official
Beatles **FAN CLUB**

45
R.P.M.

Another
Beatles Christmas Record

Above *A record was given away free every Christmas to members of the official fan club.*

Opposite page *From the Cavern Club to Buckingham Palace in three short years.*

Paul examines his medal after the investiture ceremony.

The title of the album was reportedly dreamed up by McCartney as a punning comment on the then-growing British infatuation with soul music. But 'Rubber Soul' was no slice of plagiarism: it represented a major turning point for the Beatles and for the standard of long-playing records in general.

Certainly it is flawed – but these flaws are somehow less offensive ten years later than other transgressions committed for perhaps more comprehensible reasons.

The incredibly complicated 'Drive My Car' is majestic in its tortuous key shifts, strident vocals and scintillating guitar patterns. Lennon's cutting black humour reaches an all-time vitriolic peak: the musical lustre of 'Norwegian Wood', 'Nowhere Man' and 'Girl' is equalled only by the absolute lusty viciousness of the lyrics. ('Norwegian Wood' is allegedly about a clandestine affair of Lennon's; he didn't want Cynthia, his first wife, to know, so he disguised the story line.)

In contrast, McCartney's flatulent and sugary 'Michelle' was lauded far beyond its station and finished up the most covered track on the album.

The powerful influence that George Martin had always exerted surfaces in the form of an instrumental solo on Lennon's 'In My Life': his gorgeous baroque piano lifts the number into a completely new musical context. Harrison – whose guitar work throughout is happily nothing short of superb – came up with his best song to date, 'If I Needed Someone', where the vocal line follows alternate off-beat quavers with unerring accuracy, leading to a simply glorious three-part harmony in the closing stages.

It was obvious that the group were no longer concerned with their public image as 'lovable mop tops' etc. They were Artists and, like Artists, they wanted things done their way (for the sake of the Art). 'Rubber Soul' was.

'Day Tripper' (John and Paul)/'We Can Work It Out' (Paul)
Parlophone R 5389. Produced: George Martin
Released: December 3, 1965

The Beatles, like their nearest competitors, the Rolling Stones, themed many of their early-mid-period singles upon strong, compulsive riffs. 'Day Tripper' had a riff so catchy and original (like its predecessor 'Ticket To Ride') that even US soul stylist Otis Redding felt compelled to cover it, up-tempo'd and with the Mar-keys (the Stax house band) belting out the riff Basie-fashion.

Excellent though it was, public taste – as expressed by BBC disc-jockeys – compelled EMI to flip the single in favour of the hitherto B-side, 'We Can Work It Out', only a few days after release.

This harmonium-dominated track was certainly pleasing enough, and the iron-clad harmony duo of Lennon and McCartney made short work of the minor/major modulations. The four bars which separate the two sections of the middle-eight float deftly in and out of waltz time. Further time-experiments were to follow on their next album.

'Beatles Million Sellers'
Parlophone GEP 8946. Produced: George Martin
Released: December 5, 1965
She Loves You/I Want To Hold Your Hand/Can't Buy Me Love/I Feel Fine

Just in case you'd worn out your original copies. And it *was* Christmas.

Daily Mirror
4d. Saturday, June 12, 1965 No. 19,120
Now they are in the topmost chart of all
BEATLES, MBE!

James Paul McCartney, Esq. MBE. John Winston Lennon, Esq. MBE. Richard (Ringo) Starkey, Esq. MBE. and George Harrison, Esq. MBE.

Daily Mirror
4d. Tuesday, June 15, 1965 No. 19,122
Ex-RAF man says Honour is cheapened
TWO MBEs SENT BACK BECAUSE OF BEATLES

1966

January 21
It's always the quiet blokes that pull the tastiest birds. George Harrison weds model Patricia Anne Boyd.

(Below)

May 1
Last public appearance in England (on May Day) at the *New Musical Express* Pollwinners' Concert.

June
Three-day tour of Germany. (*Bottom left and right*)

'Yesterday'
Parlophone GEP 8948. Produced: George Martin
Released: March 4, 1966
Act Naturally/You Like Me Too Much/Yesterday/It's Only Love

'Singles' in the USA translated as 'EPs' for the British and European markets.

'Paperback Writer' (Paul)/'Rain' (John)
Parlophone R 5452. Produced: George Martin
Released: June 10, 1966

Eight years after the event, opinions still differ as to the merits of 'Paperback Writer' – the first Beatles single to receive less-than-universal acclaim. Perhaps a trifle too 'clever' and over-confident, it has nonetheless matured with age and now stands as a stunning exercise in technique and a genuine search for a new direction at a time when the rush of Beatlemania was becoming an inhibiting factor in the group's creativity.

'Paperback Writer' exists because of Paul's desire to match the Beach Boys in the technique of harmony counterpoint. Objections were based upon the triviality of the lyric and a slight nagging suspicion that the Beatles were playing at 'being song writers' at a time when the world was waiting for The Word.

'Rain' is an excursion into primitive psychedelia before The Word (or its creative limits) had been defined.

'Nowhere Man'
Parlophone GEP 8952. Produced: George Martin
Released: July 8, 1966
Nowhere Man/Drive My Car/Michelle/You Won't See Me

The issue of this EP reflects a cute tactic of the mid-'sixties record companies: find out which were the most popular tracks from the artists' last LP – and presto! Another Extended-Player. An accountants' move.

The Beatles photographed at various times in 1966.

1966

June/July
Far East Tour.

August
Farewell tour of America. But nobody realised it at the time.

'The Beatles are bigger than Jesus Christ.' John Lennon, quoted by columnist Maureen Cleave in the London *Evening Standard*.

'I'm really knocked out at having three of my compositions on the "Revolver" album. It took a lot of effort, because I'm very conscious of being overpowered by John and Paul.' George Harrison.

Below John's 'blasphemous' statement causes an uproar. An American local radio station stages a public 'Beatle burning' in which its entire stock of Beatle records go up in smoke amid cheers from disillusioned fans.

Opposite page A fine, if austere, sleeve designed by bassist and artist Klaus Voormann.

REVOLVER
Parlophone PCS 7009. Produced: George Martin
Released: August 5, 1966
Taxman (George)/Eleanor Rigby (Paul)/I'm Only Sleeping (John)/Love You To (George)/ Here, There and Everywhere (Paul)/Yellow Submarine (Ringo)/She Said She Said (John)/ Good Day Sunshine (Paul)/And Your Bird Can Sing (John)/For No One (Paul)/Doctor Robert (John)/I Want To Tell You (George)/Got To Get You Into My Life (Paul)/Tomorrow Never Knows (John)

This almost flawless album can be seen as the peak of the Beatles' creative career. They were later to undertake more ambitious projects which would be crowned with equal critical acclaim, but 'Revolver' is the kind of achievement which any artist would be more than satisfied to regard as some kind of culmination to his career. No less than that.

And it could probably have only been made at this particular juncture in the Beatles' career. Touring was, for them, a bar to music; live gigs had been largely farcical affairs where even the group were unable to hear (or even care about) the quality of their performance. So 'Revolver' marks the emergence of the Beatles as a studio band purely and simply. Plus the final assembly of all their influences in one place at one time, plus the growing infatuation with drug-based ideology (and the drugs themselves), it all combined to create a pool of assets which was joyfully put to use in almost staggering fashion. Despite the brilliance evident on almost every track, there is still a strong element of disciplined understatement which had always characterised their work and which makes 'Revolver' quite timeless; unlike the later 'Sgt Pepper', it has aged well – it's even matured – and the wealth of musical invention, social observation and downright intuition are as fresh today as when the album was originally issued.

Of course, much of this appreciation is largely restrospective; at the time it was Another Beatle Album and therefore a goldmine of potential singles for other artists. So Cilla Black recorded a version of McCartney's 'For No One', and soul artist Cliff Bennett lifted the

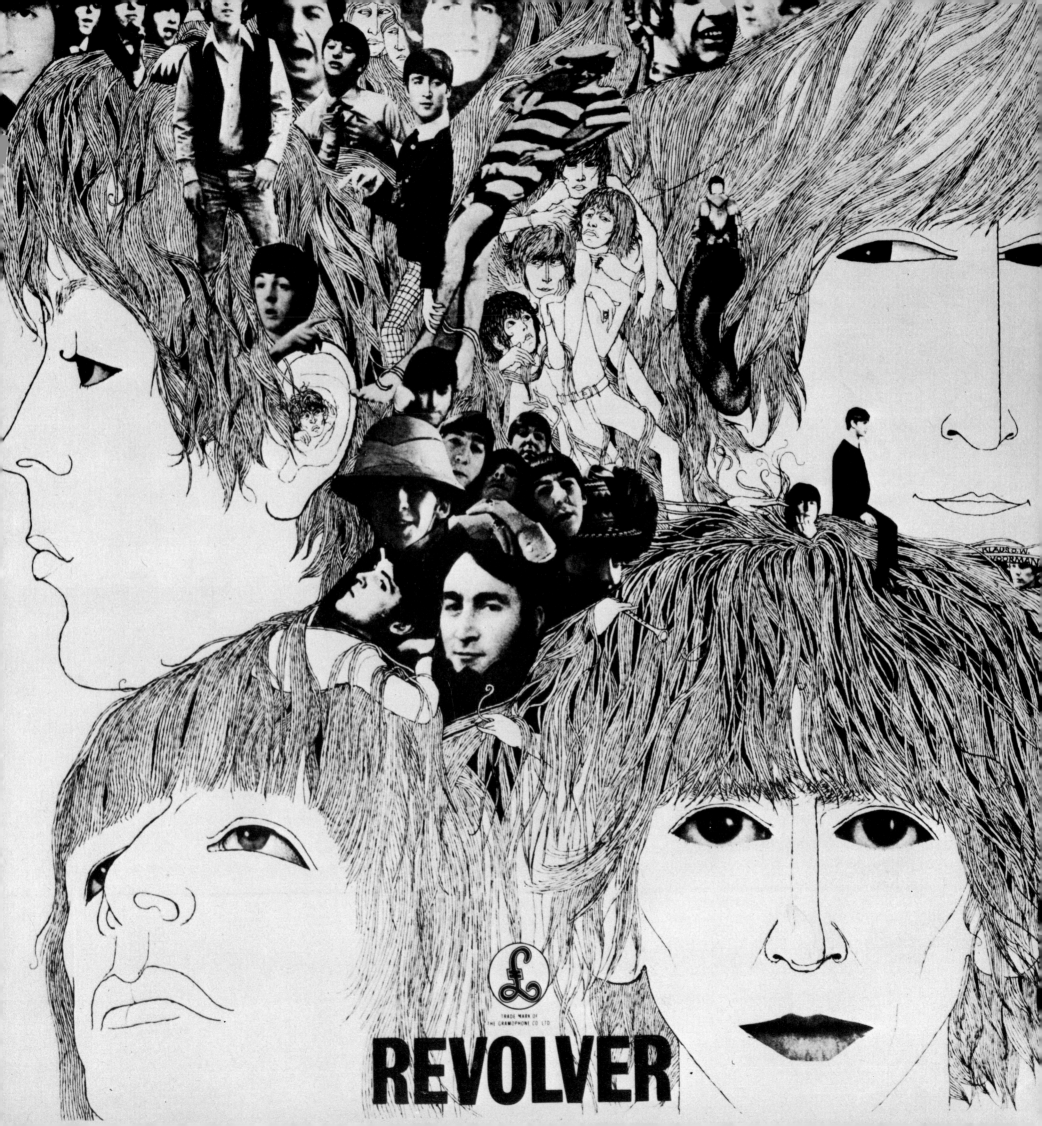

REVOLVER

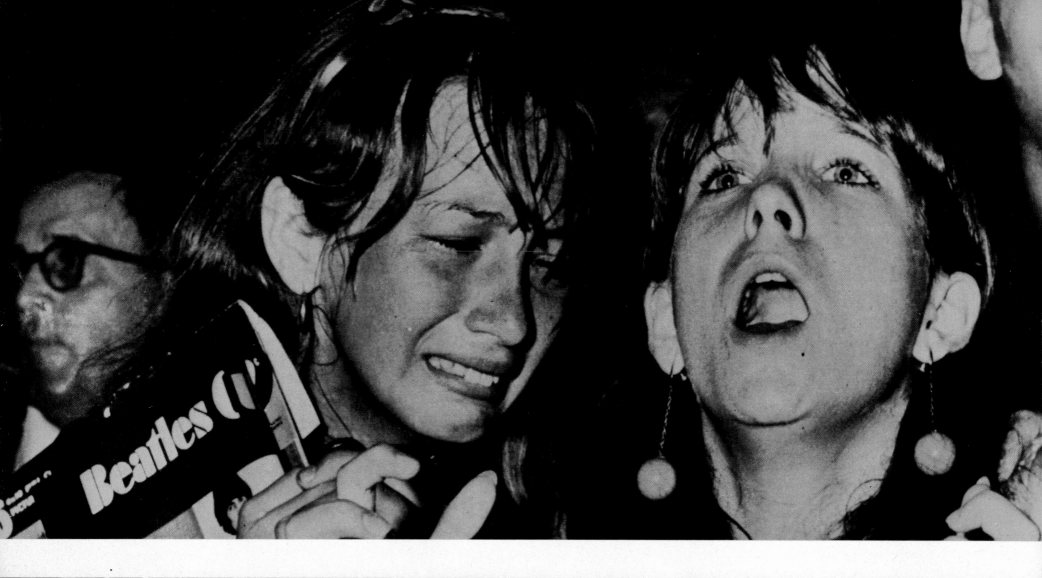

(soul-orientated) 'Got To Get You Into My Life' in best fellow-traveller fashion. But for purists the *real* versions were the Beatles' own.

Harrison, who'd had a bleak composing period at the apogee of Beatlemania, was about to enter the period of his Beatle life when he would have most influence over the other three – largely because of his discovery and subsequent devotion to Indian mysticism (itself a purist reaction to LSD and drug ideology). In fact, his Hindi-style songs (on 'Revolver' and on 'Pepper') are weak and embarrassing – but his sometime capacity for writing a powerful conventional song with excellent guitar and superb dynamics showed to advantage on 'Taxman', the first track on 'Revolver', which was a minor miracle for a George Harrison composition and one of the album's most compulsive rockers. (It also pinpointed his monetary obsessions.) 'Love You To' is Harrison's first attempt at an Indian-style tune – and it suffers for the reasons explained above. Sitars and tablas carry the tune and the rhythm. George himself, an earnest student of Indian musical forms under the tutelage of Ravi Shankar, makes sincere but inept attempts to play the solo instrumental line and reportedly spent all day trying to get both the arrangement and his own part accurate. The rented Indian tabla-wallahs easily outshine him.

Lennon's eerie and shivery 'I'm Only Sleeping', with its backward tape obbligatos (courtesy of Georges Harrison and Martin) underscored the visionary discoveries Lennon had made under the influence of the various chemicals he'd been pouring into his system with deadly regularity. It is a remarkable song (he was to continue the spooky somnambulism on a later piece, 'I'm So Tired', from 'the White Album').

The beautiful pair of McCartney songs – 'Here There and Everywhere' and 'For No One' – represent Paul at his best: melodicism to the fore, sentimentality kept to economical levels.

September/October
Lennon cuts hair for co-starring role in Dick Lester movie *How I Won the War.*

Opposite top *The Philadelphia concert, August 16, brings tears of happiness and screams of delight.*

Opposite bottom *The fans have evidently forgiven John, and thousands pack Chicago's International Amphitheatre on August 13.*

Below *John co-stars with Lee Montague in* How I Won the War.

1966

The latter piece is decorated by a superb french-horn solo from symphony-player Alan Civil (this solo was reportedly hummed by McCartney to George Martin, who instantly committed it to manuscript paper). Lennon – who throughout, reminds of his growing departure from McCartney's more lyrical style of composing – turns in three of his best tunes: 'She Said She Said', 'And Your Bird Can Sing' and 'Doctor Robert' (a paean to a pill-peddling physician).

The marvellous eclecticism of 'Revolver' was further emphasised by the inclusion of a quasi-soul number, 'Got To Get You Into My Life', sung with great gusto by Paul – and it proved that the Beatles, in addition to their other talents, were quite able to incorporate other musical forms quite effortlessly (the British music scene was currently undergoing an infatuation with soul music) and with almost contemptuous indifference.

But it is the closing track, 'Tomorrow Never Knows', which is the clincher on this collection. And a signpost for the next album. Droning sitars, backward tapes and snippets from the Tibetan Book of the Dead proclaimed that John Winston Lennon had more in common with LSD guru Timothy Leary than Caucasian ancestry and a predilection for convincing flannel.

The overall effect of 'Revolver' is majestic. A subjective opinion: the Beatles were never to surpass the standard of writing and playing which can be found on almost every track. Though Lennon himself later claimed (in a *Rolling Stone* interview) that he couldn't even remember the sessions, that seems an over-dismissive comment in view of the extraordinary respect with which this Beatle LP is treated over all others (with the possible and disputable exception of 'Sgt Pepper'). The sleeve was designed by Beatle confidant Klaus Voormann, a German bassist from Hamburg and an old friend from earlier days; it was an austere collage that did nothing to predict the lavishness of the cover on their next album.

Further interest lies in the US compilation of the same name. By dint of furious enterprise, the Americans had managed to issue eleven albums in the same period as EMI (in England) had issued seven: naturally, there were no extra tracks – just more re-issues and 'compilations'. By some inter-company scheming, Capitol (US) acquired the 'Revolver' tapes some four months earlier than the British. Three of these appear on a US collection titled 'Yesterday and Today' – 'I'm Only Sleeping', 'Doctor Robert', 'And Your Bird Can Sing' – while the US issue of 'Revolver' (in August) boasted only eleven songs (instead of fourteen on the British version). Apart from 'Magical Mystery Tour' and 'Hey Jude', all subsequent US albums corresponded exactly with their British counterparts.

'Eleanor Rigby' (Paul)/'Yellow Submarine' (Ringo)
Parlophone R 5493. Produced: George Martin
Released: August 8, 1966

This issue of this particular single underlined a growing dodge in the ever-innovative music industry. Instead of releasing the 'EP-after-the-LP', why not preview the forthcoming album with two culled tracks *as a single?*

It goes without saying that this accountants' ploy produced a certain indecision over which should be the A-side. To solve the problem, on this occasion *both* tracks were officially designated A-sides.

'Eleanor Rigby', featuring a fruity string quartet, displayed McCartney's growing desire to be taken as a 'lyricist of consequence'. Sociology, not for the first time, reared a misshapen skull. Though much praised at the time (by sociologists), 'Eleanor Rigby' was sentimental, melodramatic and a blind alley.

The reverse, 'Yellow Submarine', was acclaimed as the best kiddie-toon since Mel Blanc's 'I T'ought I T'aw a Puddytat'. Ringo yodelled it while John clanged bells and made absurd U-boat noises. It seems ridiculous now – it seemed ridiculous then – but it sold well, which justified the EMI accountants at the next policy meeting.

58

October
Harrison visits Bombay and partakes of his first cosmic curry.

December
Sessions commence for what is to become the 'Sgt Pepper' LP.

Right *Old favourites in place of new product this Christmas.*

Below *John with George Martin in the studio – 'Sgt Pepper' in the making.*

A COLLECTION OF OLDIES ... BUT GOLDIES
Parlophone PCS 7016. Produced: George Martin
Released: November 1966
She Loves You/From Me To You/We Can Work It Out/Help!/Michelle/Yesterday/I Feel Fine/Yellow Submarine/Can't Buy Me Love/Bad Boy/Day Tripper/A Hard Day's Night/ Ticket To Ride/Paperback Writer/Eleanor Rigby/I Want To Hold Your Hand

Once again, it was Christmas – and the Beatles had *no new product* to give to EMI for their Santa sack! As a last resort, a predictable collection of oldies was hastily assembled and crammed into an inferior Carnaby-Street-style carrier-bag sleeve.

The only all-new track – which had been released in the USA in June 1965 on 'Beatles VI' – was Larry Williams' 'Bad Boy'.

59

THE STUDIO

1967

February
The Harrison's first contact with the mysticism of the East — in the person of transcendental mystic Maharishi Mahesh Yogi. The Beatles are now completely studio-orientated, having retired from touring and eschewed all personal appearances. 'Penny Lane'/'Strawberry Fields' fails to reach Number One in singles chart.

A studio session for 'Sgt Pepper'.

'Penny Lane' (Paul)/'Strawberry Fields Forever' (John)
Parlophone R 5570. Produced: George Martin
Released: February 17, 1967

Both these tracks represent definitive English acid-rock (as opposed to its American cousin), full of arpeggio trumpets, ever-faithful backward tapes, surging strings, surreal lyrics, fade-outs, fade-ins, false endings, mysterious mutterings, hypnotic, insistent drumming, jokes galore and almost endless ambiguities.

The subject-matter was essentially 'Liverpool-on-a-sunny-hallucinogenic-afternoon'. It was a studio record masterfully produced on both sides and, as usual, a classy encapsulation of a whole mood then prevalent among the people who bought the Beatles' records. And yet this double A-side only reached the number two spot in the national charts, thus provoking the predictable 'Are the Beatles slipping?' speculations in the press.

The best in this vein was still to come.

Left *George Martin, in the role of Beatles' record producer, played an important part in their musical development, particularly during their 'studio years'.*

Top left *John and Ringo listen to a playback of 'Sgt Pepper's Lonely Hearts Club Band'.*

Above *Paul conducting a forty-one-piece orchestra, 1967. (Mick Jagger sits at his feet.) Orchestras and advanced production techniques were typical of the Beatles' recordings at this time.*

1967

Sgt PEPPER'S LONELY HEARTS CLUB BAND
Parlophone PCS 7027. Produced: George Martin
Released: June 1, 1967
Sgt Pepper's Lonely Hearts Club Band (Paul and John)/With a Little Help From My Friends (Ringo)/Lucy In the Sky With Diamonds (John)/Getting Better (Paul)/Fixing a Hole (Paul)/She's Leaving Home (Paul)/Being For The Benefit Of Mr Kite (John)/Within You, Without You (George)/When I'm Sixty Four (Paul)/Lovely Rita (Paul)/Good Morning, Good Morning (John)/A Day In the Life (John and Paul)

Five years ago this day, George Martin told the Beatles, 'Play!' – and who could have predicted it would come to this? 'Sgt Pepper' is surely the Beatles' greatest technical achievement and, if hindsight reveals many of the contrivances, they weren't in any way apparent in June 1967, high-water-mark of the psychedelic era.

Where 'Revolver' left off, 'Sgt Pepper' begins: it's a stupefying collage of music, words, background noises, cryptic utterances, orchestral effects, hallucinogenic bells, farmyard sounds, dream sequences, social observations and apocalyptic vision, all masterfully blended together on a four-track tape machine over nine agonising and expensive months. 'Pepper'

June 1
The release of 'Sgt Pepper's Lonely Hearts Club Band' album and the Dawn of a New Era. Controversy rages over 'overt drug allusions' in 'A Day in the Life', which is subsequently banned by the BBC and some US stations.

Below left The Beatles all grew moustaches for 'Sgt Pepper'.

Opposite page The 'Sgt Pepper' sleeve, designed by British pop artists Peter Blake and Jan Haworth.

Below Examples of the original artwork for the sleeve.

June 25
'All You Need Is Love' recorded live direct from EMI's London studio as part of a worldwide television transmission during the programme 'Our World'. Viewers estimated at about 150,000,000, and song puts Beatles back at Number One in singles chart.

August 8
George Harrison pays surprise visit to San Francisco's hippieland, Haight-Asbury.

Above left *George with Derek Taylor in San Francisco.*

Above right *The Beatles and friends (Mick Jagger at far right) with the Maharishi (centre) and followers at Bangor.*

Left *'All You Need Is Love'* TV *broadcast.*

reputedly cost £40,000 to make – as will be observed, a far cry from the budget restrictions of the 'Please Please Me' collection. Its concept formula expanded the entire horizon of pop album structure, although it still boiled down to a selection of twelve songs plus a reprise of the title track. This 'concept', sold with the aid of its extraordinarily lavish gatefold sleeve, escalated the business of LP recording and marketing into a kind of album race with groups vieing with each other to see who could spend more money and take more time over their next presentation.

'Pepper' was the first of these spectaculars – and is also the best, though its imperfections have aged badly, probably due to the overall self-consciousness with which ex-hippies now view their immediate past. But like 'The Bhagavad-Gita' and 'The Lord of The Rings', it is inextricably associated with that past.

The title track appears in two forms: the longer, more grandiose version opens the album; the reprise – shorter, brisker, and punchier – heralds the final track. Brass bands and crowd noises plus whining guitar segue* from the beginning into one of the Beatles' major compositions of this period, 'With a Little Help From My Friends', on which Ringo's homely voice provides just the right degree of bathos to off-set the potential sentimentality of the lyric. (This tune incidentally provided British soul shouter Joe Cocker with what most critics accept as the best-ever interpretation of a Lennon/McCartney original.)

Lennon's 'Lucy In the Sky With Diamonds' has long been the subject of conjecture: the significant initials LSD, and the overt hallucinogenic inspirations provided fuel for those who accused the Beatles of inducing others to take drugs. Lennon has always denied this.

McCartney's 'Getting Better' and 'Fixing a Hole' are slow and fast versions respectively of the same song and strongly reflect his ascendant middle-class optimism. 'She's Leaving Home' shows the more sentimental side of his essentially bourgeois talent; it is one of the songs on 'Pepper' that has failed to mature and, although beautifully crafted (especially in the juxtaposition of lead and backing vocals), now stands revealed as a shameless tear-jerker. Lennon's 'Mr Kite' again reveals John as a mischievous psychedelicatessen: cascading calliopes and celestes recapture the surreal atmosphere of the carnival. Lennon later confessed that the seemingly cryptic lyric was, in fact, culled from a decorative circus poster.

Side Two of 'Sgt Pepper' opens with the album's nadir, the Indianesque 'Within You, Without You', composed, played and sung by George Harrison. It is nothing more than a vibed-up remake of 'Love You To' (from 'Revolver'), and no more adventurous than the average soundtrack on a *very* average Bombay-produced movie.

The next track, 'When I'm Sixty Four', shows, with fantastic incongruity, McCartney's sometimes-regrettable penchant for vaudeville. The soft-shoe shuffle – music to tap-dance by – may have fitted the 'Pepper' concept, but it was quite traumatic after the bejewelled pretentiousness of Harrison's preceding devotional. However, McCartney slips neatly back into focus with a charming piece of lampoonery, 'Lovely Rita', directed at female traffic-wardens (who have been known in Britain as meter maids ever since).

'Good Morning, Good Morning', which segues into the 'Pepper' reprise, is the album's most disposable track. Sure, it fills a hole where the rain got in but the emptiness of the inspiration is further emphasised by the smothering brass of Sounds Inc – and the trick, already used on the Beach Boys 'Pet Sounds' LP, of featuring farmyard animal noises to conceal the fact that no ending had actually been worked out.

It is the extraordinary finale, 'A Day In the Life', which commands most attention. In origin, it was two separate songs – but Lennon's had no middle and McCartney's had no beginning, so the two were skilfully fused together to create what is one of the great studio masterpieces of the era: a piece of music which has been interpreted as no less than a vision of the Day of Judgment. Lennon, already the most misinterpreted Beatle (his 'Jesus Christ' quote had never been forgiven in certain sections of America's Bible Belt) found his arch use of imagery and his free lateral association widely viewed as a clarion call to do whatever the

* Segue: to phase from one tune into another with no discernible pause.

1967

August 27
Smartly kaftanned — and carrying bouquets of flowers — all four Beatles and their chums seek divine guidance from the Maharishi among the metal-framed chairs at the Teachers' Training College in Bangor, North Wales. The news of manager Brian Epstein's death breaks up the soirée.

'I've not taken any drugs since we started on this meditation. I hope I will get so much out of this I will not have to go back on drugs.' Ringo Starr.

'The taking of drugs expands the consciousness. But it's like taking an aspirin without having a headache.' Paul McCartney.

John and the Maharishi in the train for Bangor.

Top *This is the last photograph of Brian Epstein with the Beatles – he died in August.*

Above *Another powerful Eastern influence was Indian musician Ravi Shankar.*

aggrieved listener secretly wanted to do most of all. McCartney's coy references to pot-smoking – although originally meant for a different song – seemed to add weight to this theory. And the cataclysmic orchestral build-up, which occurs twice, was widely taken as being intended to simulate the 'rush' which occurs with the use of certain drugs. Others interpreted the very same orchestral effect as a prophecy of Armageddon. If so, the extended piano chord – which puts the seal on both song and album – comes across with all the morbid majesty of a slamming sarcophagus lid.

Mystery still surrounds 'Sergeant Pepper'. It was so intended. Infallible rumour suggests it was originally conceived as a double album, but time and finance (in the form of horrified EMI auditors) finally intervened and 'Pepper' emerged in the form in which we know it. Speculation was rife as to the message intended by the enigmatic sleeve photo (for the next three years all Beatle albums were similarly searched for hidden meaning). And much furore was generated by the display, in the photo-spread, of a thriving bed of cannabis plants.

The Beatles all grew moustaches.

'All You Need Is Love' (John)/'Baby You're a Rich Man' (Paul)
Parlophone R 5620. Produced: George Martin
Released: July 7, 1967

In keeping with their new-found roles as everybody's favourite gurus, the Beatles cast feverishly around for something significant to say . . . and, instead, took refuge in a fabulous piece of self-satire.

Even today (1974) it's impossible to hear the opening bars of the French national anthem without instinctively lurching into the Beatles' all-time kitsch peace anthem 'All You Need Is Love'. Thus they injected a vital element of self-parody into a lumbering, decorated-but-dour-with-it Love Generation. The reformed hippie now winces at his own ludicrous past but he can bellow tunelessly along with this glorious, irreverent single *without any real embarrassment* – a measure of its internal strength and durability.

'Baby You're a Rich Man' is another psychedelic throw-away, notable only for ridiculously speeded-up trumpet obbligatos.

The Beatles re-appear (bottom) in the collarless suits beloved of fans in those early days. This apparent movement into the past was not just nostalgia – they are dressed this way for a short BBC TV film planned to coincide with the release of 'Hello, Goodbye'. The photograph below really was taken in 1963.

Magical Mystery Tour sleeve. This is the American LP, not the British EP.

'Hello Goodbye' (Paul)/'I Am the Walrus' (John)
Parlophone R 5655. Produced: George Martin
Released: November 14, 1967

Lyrical obscurity rears a puzzled head in the last of the Beatles' psychedelic singles. 'Hello Goodbye' showcases McCartney being clever with paradoxical statements, while the reverse . . .

MAGICAL MYSTERY TOUR
Parlophone SMMT 1/2. Produced: George Martin
Released: December 1967
Magical Mystery Tour (John and Paul)/Your Mother Should Know (Paul)/I Am the Walrus (John)/Fool On the Hill (Paul)/Flying (instrumental)/Blue Jay Way (George)

The Beatles' disappointing TV fantasy produced a comparatively paltry collection of songs – in the unusual form of a double EP set complete with presentation book. The Americans, true to form, contrived to squeeze an LP out of the same tracks, adding 'Hello Goodbye', 'Strawberry Fields Forever', 'Penny Lane', 'Baby You're a Rich Man' and 'All You Need

69

1967

Below *'All You Need Is Love'* in four languages. Or is it?

Is Love'. Two recorded tracks – 'Shirley's Wild Accordion' and 'Jessie's Dream' – never made it on to wax in any form at all.

It's a fairly discouraging set. By far the most outstanding cuts are McCartney's exquisite 'Fool On the Hill' and Lennon's downright peculiar 'I Am the Walrus', which features him at a surrealistic zenith. The insistent and ominous two-note base for the tune was inspired by a police car siren which caused Lennon considerable paranoia one night in New York. And nobody has yet managed to convey what the lyrics *mean* – Lennon himself has admitted absolute ignorance. 'Your Mother Should Know' displays regrettable McCartney vaudeville, and the monotonous 'Blue Jay Way' indicates Harrison's paucity of ideas when deprived of Hindu support.

Nobody liked the film either.

September/November *Magical Mystery Tour*, conceived originally for the Big Screen as a reaction to the cardboard *Help!* ('We can make a much better movie ourselves'; ends up on TV and is slaughtered by public and critics alike. But it was a brave attempt. December Ringo seems not at all inhibited while filming *Candy* with Brando and Burton.	December 7 Grand opening of ill-fated Beatles' Apple Shop at 94 Baker Street. December 25 Paul McCartney and Jane Asher announce engagement. December 26 World première of *Magical Mystery Tour* on BBC-1. Happy Christmas.

Above *John and a clown at the opening of the Apple Shop.*

Right & opposite page *Enter the 'Egg Men'. Scenes from the film* Magical Mystery Tour.

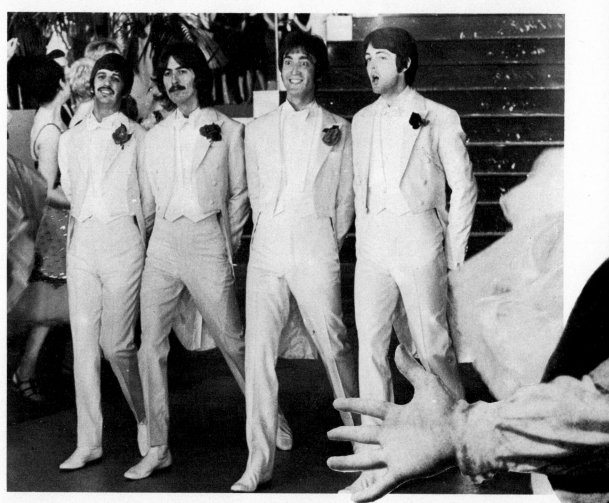

1968

The Beatles (minus Ringo) with their girl friends and the Maharishi at Rishikesh. Also present are Mia Farrow and Donovan.

January 5
Despite unanimous thumbs-down, *Magical Mystery Tour* gets a second showing – this time in colour – on BBC-2.

January
George back in Bombay, 'Wonder-walling' with local musicians.

February/April
Beatles under spell of bearded silver-tongued Swami at Maharishi's Academy at Rishikesh, India. This establishment described as: 'Just like Butlin's' by down-to-earth Ringo. Yogi (allegedly) tries his luck and gets less-than-holy with Mia Farrow, and rest of Beatles depart for London.

'Lady Madonna' (Paul)/'The Inner Light' (George)
Parlophone R 5675. Produced: George Martin
Released: March 15, 1968

The appearance of 'Lady Madonna' indicates the Indian Summer of the Beatles as singles artists. The recent spate of magnificent albums seemed to have lessened the group's desire to put real effort into what seemed, at the time, to be an outmoded recording medium. And, since the death of Brian Epstein six months earlier, Paul McCartney – whose particular instant-melody talents had always lain more with the three-minute song – had come more and more to the fore. He wrote 'Lady Madonna' and all the remaining singles except for Lennon's 'Ballad of John and Yoko' and Harrison's 'Something' (itself taken from the 'Abbey Road' album).

McCartney had always been ready and willing to step into any leadership gaps: from the beginning, Brian Epstein himself had noticed this eager quality of Paul's and had tried to channel it. With Epstein's death, McCartney took a temporary leading role, which owed as much to Lennon's abdication as to Paul's qualities.

Nevertheless, 'Lady Madonna' is a fine single and, like all their truly historic short tracks, features several new experiments: in this case, dependence on a powerful riff from a horn section (led by jazz musician Ronnie Scott) and on the use of McCartney's own ability to vary his 'voices'. He employed a Presley baritone on this Fats Domino-inspired boogie.

The middle-eight features the Beatles' supreme qualities as backing vocalists – an infrequently praised talent – and the words were as mysterious as any Beatleologist could wish. Who was Lady Madonna? Surely the Beatles were not urging Roman Catholicism upon us? No, it *had* to be a gag. Or did it? You never knew after all, and it was not unknown for people to be caught playing the labels (or even the sleeves) of Beatle records in order to find

Revelation.

They *believed* in gurus in those days.

Fats Domino himself paid the totally appropriate compliment of covering this track – along with Joe Cocker's version of 'A Little Help From My Friends', surely one of the superior Beatle interpretations. But Domino had been an early influence, after all.

The reverse side, 'The Inner Light', is a feeble transcendental tune from George Harrison, at this time securely under the influence of the Maharishi.

'Hey Jude' (Paul)/'Revolution' (John)
Apple R 5722. Produced: George Martin
Released: August 30, 1968

The death of Brian Epstein liberated the Beatles from his kindly leadership. One of their first independent acts was to set up their own organisation – to release their own material, to discover and promote other artists and to be a general idealistic stimulus to a music industry which the Beatles, now in their greatest idealistic period, considered jaded and in great need of non-materialistic dialectic.

The story of Apple is in fact not a happy one, but the first release on the new label, 'Hey Jude', promised great things. The second of the McCartney-dominated singles (and the last great Beatles single recorded *specifically* for the 45s market) was incidentally the last occasion when they would appear on (British) TV to promote a new recording. The David Frost programme was transformed into a real beanfeast by the marathon length and anthem structure of 'Hey Jude'; it was a genuinely warm and moving occasion and the ten-mile fade-out set yet another innovatory trend – with other artists apeing the epic proportions of the piece but failing to capture the gentleness and sympathy of the Beatles' communal feel.

The message-analysers (now in full cry) read an appeal directed at Bob Dylan into the lyric; naturally, the Beatles denied it. They also denied that 'Hey Jude' was dedicated to a certain lady Fleet Street Showbiz columnist, affectionately known as 'Fag-ash Lil'.

The B-side now greatly contrasts with some of the more extreme political attitudes later adopted by Lennon; at this time, actionism was uncool and Lennon's lyric firmly puts the knife into any hopes that politicos might entertain of the Beatles lending prestige to the Demo movement.

WONDERWALL MUSIC
Apple SAPCOR 1. Produced: George Harrison
Released: November 1, 1968
Microbes/Red Lady Too/Tabla and Pakavaj/In the Park/Drilling a Home/Guru Vandana/Greasy Legs/Ski-ing/Gat Kirwani/Dream Scene/Party Seacombe/Love Scene/Crying/Cowboy Music/Fantasy Sequins/On the Bed/Glass Box/Wonderwall To Be Here/Singing Om

The first solo endeavour by any Beatle, and the first album released on their much-heralded Apple project. It deserved better than this undistinguished film muzak sampler.

The only occasions on which real music manages to surface are the results of the December '67 Bombay sessions, featuring Ashish Khan on sarod; but these have little to do with Harrison and it is the musicians' own excellence which salvages the general disorganisation of the LP. It was, after all, soundtrack music – yet Harrison seemingly did not flinch from some hideous incongruities. It doesn't stand on its own but then maybe it wasn't really meant to . . . the film, by all accounts, was equally undistinguished. A poor LP start for Apple.

Wonderwall Music By George Harrison   Apple Recor

Top 'Hey Jude' performed on the Frost Show.   Right *The first Beatle solo album.*

1968

April
Apple Corps launched – Savile Row takes on new look, and No. 3 rapidly becomes Mecca for international wasters, posers and rip-off artists.

July 17
Yellow Submarine surfaces for world première at London Pavilion.

August
Paul McCartney and Jane Asher call it quits.

October
John and Yoko busted by drug squad.

November 8
John and Cynthia also call it quits. In the divorce court.

John and Paul at the Apple Press conference in New York.

74

'THE BEATLES' (the 'White Album')
Apple PCS 7067/68 Produced: George Martin
Released: November 1968
Back In the USSR (Paul)/Dear Prudence (John)/Glass Onion (John)/Ob-la-di, Ob-la-da (Paul)/Wild Honey Pie (Paul)/The Continuing Story Of Bungalow Bill (John)/While My Guitar Gently Weeps (George)/Happiness Is a Warm Gun (John)/Martha My Dear (Paul)/ I'm So Tired (John)/Blackbird (Paul)/Piggies (George)/Rocky Raccoon (Paul)/Don't Pass Me By (Ringo)/Why Don't We Do It In the Road (John and Paul)/I Will (Paul)/Julia (John)/ Birthday (Paul)/Yer Blues (John)/Mother Nature's Son (Paul)/Everybody's Got Something To Hide Except Me and My Monkey (John)/Sexy Sadie (John)/Helter Skelter (Paul)/Long Long Long (George)/Revolution 1 (John)/Honey Pie (Paul)/Savoy Truffle (George)/Cry Baby Cry (John)/Revolution 9 (instrumental)/Goodnight (Ringo)

The Beatles' decision to release their first *real* album after 'Sgt Pepper' in a plain white sleeve (in contrast to the lavishness of the latter cover) indicated more than a sudden desire for austerity: the 'White Album' – as it became rapidly known – also indicated the passing of the Beatles *as a group* and the termination of any real desire to feed ideas into a communal pool. On this double LP, *they each act as each others' session men*; didacticism is rampant and it is more of a selection of solo tracks that we hear.

'The White Album' is an odd, patchy collection: informed critics opine that there is enough material here to make one really good single album. Certainly many of the tracks are dispensable, but the best are easily as good as anything they'd done, and it is to these that any review must address itself.

McCartney's material reveals the eclecticism which had always dogged him – but this time to creditable effect. From the Beach Boys/Chuck Berry-styled opener 'Back In the USSR' (one of the best Beatle rockers ever written) to the whimsy of 'Martha My Dear' and the curious but extremely beautiful 'Blackbird' (held by many to be a sympathetic gesture towards the then-emergent Black Power movement), he hardly ever falters on this album, except on those tracks which are obvious inclusions for the sake of filling the enormous recording commitment necessitated by any double LP. His rooty-toot persona whisks past in the form of 'Rocky Raccoon' (a Mack Sennett movie set to music) and 'Honey Pie', a speak-easy special with charming flapper overtones. And nobody but McCartney could get away with the closing track, 'Goodnight', a great potential ad that Horlicks never used.

On the other hand, Lennon's unhappiness and resurgent iconoclasm come through powerfully. Swinging wildly (but sometimes accurately) at almost everything in sight, he scores telling hits on the Hippie Heaven of '67 ('Glass Onion'), a white hunter he'd met in Africa ('Bungalow Bill'), America's National Rifle Association ('Happiness Is a Warm Gun'), the British Blues Boom ('Yer Blues'), the Maharishi ('Sexy Sadie') and activists everywhere ('Revolution 1'). He attacks his own background even more strongly on 'Julia', a wistful blueprint for his later primal-scream recorded histrionics. Lennon's best song on the album is the magnificent 'I'm So Tired', almost a direct continuation of the dream-sequence commenced with 'I'm Only Sleeping' on the 'Revolver' LP. The voice control and dynamics displayed on the later bars of each verse are quite astounding and reveal him as by far the most gifted vocalist in the group.

George Harrison, a lesser composer but a better instrumentalist, has one really great moment on 'The White Album': 'While My Guitar Gently Weeps' is a majestic, bluesy piece of epic proportions and an absolute gift to a member of the guitar freemasonry then emerging, Eric Clapton, a close friend of Harrison's, who overlaid his impeccable solo on Harrison's rhythm work with his usual taste and style. It is an extraordinarily dramatic song – yet somehow never reaches the climax that it needs in order to qualify as an all-time Beatle masterpiece. Harrison's other songs, unfortunately, can be filed under 'forgettable'. 'Piggies' is nihilistic and sweeping in its condemnation of approximately half the human race – in curious contrast to his recent obsessions with universal peace and brotherly mysticism.

(The infamous Charles Manson, the American ritual murderer, is reported to have taken 'Piggies' – and McCartney's 'Helter Skelter' – as some kind of a rationale for his atrocious actions.)

The single-that-never-was – which can be found on *every* Beatle LP – is, in this case, 'Ob-la-di, Ob-la-da', a tongue-in-cheek McCartney nod in the reggae direction which was covered by the Scottish group Marmalade to their instant profit. But this – and the other undeniably superb tracks – didn't prevent the general critical opinion towards the album adding up to a consensus that, well . . . it was OK, but it was also something of a comedown after 'Pepper'. (Nowadays critics are inclined to reverse these opinions.)

The brilliance was certainly there but the Beatle Dream was almost over and, try as they might, they couldn't prevent an uncomfortable amount of the sordid world outside from creeping in.

They were no longer invulnerable.

UNFINISHED MUSIC NO. 1 –TWO VIRGINS
Apple SAPCOR 2. Produced: John Lennon and Yoko Ono
Released: November 29, 1968
Two Virgins No. 1/Together/Two Virgins No. 2/Two Virgins No. 3/Two Virgins No. 4/Two Virgins No. 5/Two Virgins No. 6/Hushabye, Hushabye/Two Virgins No. 7/Two Virgins No. 8/ Two Virgins No. 9/Two Virgins No. 10.

Unfortunately, this is even more undistinguished than 'Wonderwall'. At the least, it revealed Lennon in his true political colours: i.e. bollock-naked. Needless to say, the sleeve was banned. EMI predictably refused to distribute, so Track Records did the honours (under a plain brown wrapper). Such a big fuss over such a small thing.

'We started the album at midnight', revealed John, 'and finished it at dawn. Then we made love . . . it was very beautiful.' And Paul McCartney, still primly Y-fronted, added; 'When two great Saints meet it is a humbling experience'.

The album consists of a disjointed series of bird-calls, gastric accidents (in stereo), Yoko Ono squalling, pub piano, slowed-down tapes and other priceless recollections. What was it all trying to prove?

Apple Receptionist: *'There's an Adolf Hitler in reception.'*
Derek Taylor – Apple Press Officer: *'Oh Christ, not that arsehole again! All right, send him up!'*

'I never made any money out of the Beatles' success. I just got my same EMI *salary and never participated in their huge profits. No one could say I rode on the backs of the Beatles.'*
George Martin.

November 29
The sight of John and Yoko naked on the cover of the 'Two Virgins' album causes old ladies to reach for smelling salts.

Above *'Two Virgins' sleeve. Full frontals weren't quite such a common sight in 1968.*

Left *John and Yoko struggle towards their car, escorted by sixteen policemen, after their appearance at Marylebone Magistrates' Court.*

1968

YELLOW SUBMARINE
Apple PCS 7070. Produced: George Martin
Released: December 1968
Yellow Submarine (Ringo)/Only a Northern Song (George)/All Together Now (John, Paul, George and Ringo)/Hey, Bulldog (John)/It's All Too Much (George)/All You Need Is Love (John)
 The George Martin Orchestra: Pepperland/Sea Of Time/Sea Of Holes/Sea Of Monsters/March Of the Meanies/Pepperland Laid Waste/Yellow Submarine In Pepperland.

The Beatles, in fact, had little or nothing to do with the making of the full-length cartoon – this is indicated by the inclusion of only four new songs on what would have made a superb EP. The record business being what it is, and the film being a howling success, these four ('Only a Northern Song', 'All Together Now', 'Hey Bulldog' and 'It's All Too Much') were fleshed-out to LP proportions by 'Yellow Submarine' itself, the perennial 'All You Need Is Love' and an entire second side devoted to George Martin's soundtrack scores. By far the best of the four was Lennon's heavy-metal 'Hey, Bulldog'.

This page *'Yellow Submarine': record sleeve and stills from the film.*

Opposite page *Give-away photos from the 'White Album'.*

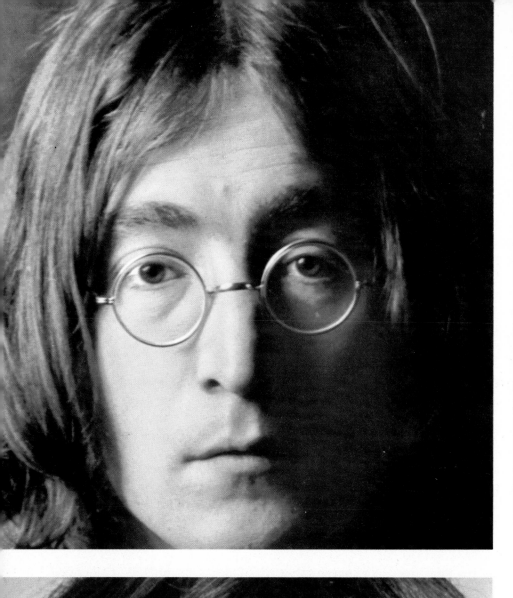

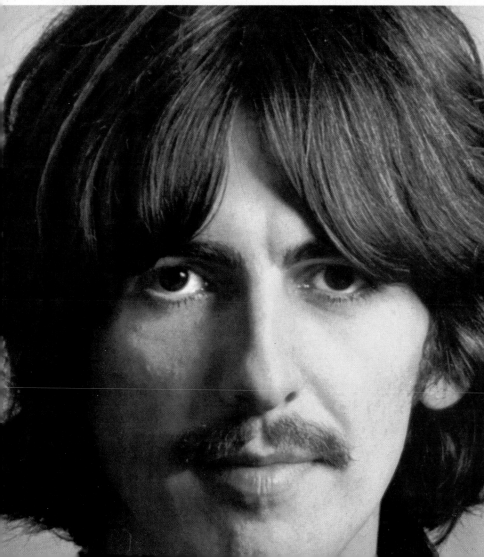
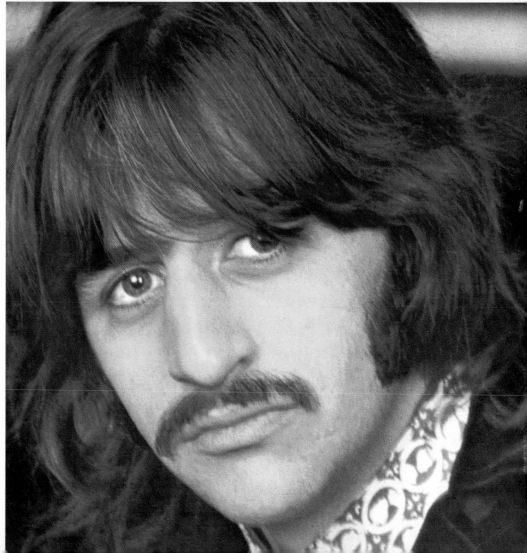

1969

January
Beatles commence work at Twickenham Studios on what is to become both an aural and visual epitaph to their existence – *Let It Be*.

January 30
Beatles put on a free lunchtime show on the roof of Apple and record 'Get Back'. Stephen King, Esq., chief accountant at the Royal Bank of Scotland (directly opposite), is Not Amused. (*Below*)

February 3
Apple Press Office release: 'The Beatles have asked Mr Allen Klein of New York to look into all their affairs and he has agreed to do so.'

'Give Peace a Chance'/'Remember Love'
Apple 13. Produced: John Lennon and Yoko Ono
Released: April 7, 1969

Lennon's latent ability to coin effective slogans emerges on this, his and Yoko's first Peace single – 'live' from yet another bed (Toronto). Although John was, at this time, riddled with media flak from surly and cynical public commentators, his fine qualities of positivism and unsinkability emerged on this appealing little anthem which was joyfully adopted by those whose politics thrive on slogans, whether positive or not.

'Get Back' (Paul)/'Don't Let Me Down' (John)
Apple R 5777. Produced: George Martin
Released: April 15, 1969

Culled from the Apple rooftop 'live' session during the filming for *Let It Be*, this stomper continued the series of McCartney-written bona-fide Beatles singles – as opposed to disguised solo excursions.

It was a superb piece of pure rock 'n' roll, featuring Lennon on lead guitar and American soul instrumentalist Billy Preston on electronic keyboards. At the time there were strong rumours that Preston would be permanently incorporated into the group (they took the unprecedented step of giving him a special name-check on the label).

McCartney's lyric for the song is typically ambiguous – references to drugs and transvestism allegedly abound – but the real meat lies in the sheer power of the performance, giving the lie to funk-obsessed Beatle critics who'd claimed the band weren't up to playing *real* rock 'n' roll.

The B-side, 'Don't Let Me Down', is a superb sober from misery-expert J. W. O. Lennon MBE. And still one of the most highly rated Beatle underbellies.

'UNFINISHED MUSIC NO. 2/LIFE WITH THE LIONS'
Zapple 01. Produced: John Lennon and Yoko Ono
Released: May 2, 1969
Cambridge 1969 (Yoko) No Bed For Beatle John (Yoko)/Baby's Heartbeat/Two Minutes Silence/Radio Play

There is much personal tragedy behind the release of this album – as the harrowing sleeve photos surely reveal. The front cover shows the Ono-Lennons in London's Queen Charlotte Hospital shortly after the loss by miscarriage of their expected child. The back picture, snapped by an alert *Daily Mirror* cameraman, reveals the smug bullying tactics of the English police around the end of the 'sixties: no less than fourteen large policemen to arrest Beatle John and his weeping Japanese wife. But Lennon, as always, stands tall . . . perhaps in the inner knowledge that the sainthood he coveted had been brought decidedly nearer by the martyrdom he'd been seeking.

It would be nice to record that this album is chockful of great music; unfortunately, such is not the case.

Side One is a curious cacophony from Cambridge, recorded March 2, 1969, in the Lady Mitchell Hall; it featured leading free-form jazz musicians John Tchikai (saxophone) and John Stevens (percussion); Lennon adds feedback guitar and Yoko belts out her breathless Banzai banalities. Side Two was recorded at Yoko's bedside on a cassette in November, 1968. Only pain *aficionados* need bother.

'The Ballad Of John and Yoko' (John)/'Old Brown Shoe' (George)
Apple R 5786. Produced: George Martin
Released: May 30, 1969

The Beatles found the world of 1969 a markedly less sympathetic place. There was much new impatience around; even lovable antics can irritate . . . after a while. John's increasing flirtations with the *avant garde* (as personified for him by Yoko Ono) had already caused some friction within the band. George is alleged to have told Yoko (to her face) that his New York friends had reported her as a woman with an over-sized ego: a bearer of bad vibes, no less.

Public feeling was even stronger. Official society arrested Lennon for possession of cannabis, and 'ex-Beatle fans', as they signed themselves, wrote charming letters to John denouncing his racial treachery (in living with a Japanese) and degenerate ways.

In reply, he and McCartney concocted this pleasant if somewhat self-pitying cantina bop. Uncomplimentary references to Jesus Christ earned him the privilege of an air-play veto in many States of the Union; but Lennon's approach to recording was currently that of the pamphleteer – his prodigious output meant little time for properly organised studio sessions. Only he and McCartney were available to play on 'The Ballad Of John and Yoko'.

ELECTRONIC SOUNDS
Zapple 02. Produced: George Harrison
Released: May 2, 1969
Under the Mersey Wall/No Time Or Space

The intended function of the (short lived) Zapple label was to be an 'artistic' outlet for the *avant garde*. Aside from the releases from the Lennons and George Harrison, plans to release a spoken word album by Ken Kesey, an album of the location performances of Lenny Bruce at the Establishment and various other similar endeavours never materialised, and the entire project was quietly abandoned.

February 4
Beatles appoint Eastman & Eastman – New York lawyers – as general consul to Apple. Let battle commence.

February 24
Triumph Investment obtain control of NEMS.

February
The Magic Christian teams Ringo with Peter Sellers.

March 12
Paul McCartney, musician, marries Linda Eastman, photographer.

Below left The sleeve for 'Unfinished Music No. 2' shows Yoko photographed in hospital after her miscarriage.

Below Paul weds Linda. The others present are, left to right: the registrar and witnesses Mal Evans and Mike McGear. The latter, a member of the Scaffold, is Paul's brother.

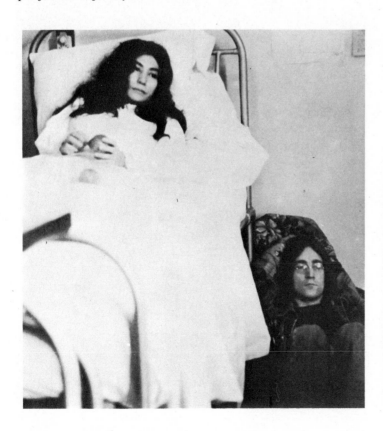

1969

March 13
George Harrison and wife Patti Boyd busted by detectives with labrador dogs at their Esher home for possessing a quantity of cannabis resin. They're each fined £250 with costs. (*Below*)

March 20
John Lennon weds Yoko Ono on the Rock of Gibraltar. (*Bottom*)

Right *A nice use of soft focus for faces no longer quite so young.*

Opposite page *The enigmatic 'Abbey Road' sleeve.*

'Electronic Music' is a very much out-of-character release from George Harrison. 'Under the Mersey Wall', which was put together in the guitarist's Esher home, and 'No Time Or Space', which materialised during a Californian vacation, manifest as nothing more invigorating than deep space static and radiophonic rejects.

ABBEY ROAD
Apple PCS 7088. Produced: George Martin
Released: September 26, 1969
Come Together (John)/Something (George)/Maxwell's Silver Hammer (Paul)/Oh! Darling (Paul)/Octopus's Garden (Ringo)/I Want You – She's So Heavy (John)/Here Comes the Sun (George)/Because (John, Paul and George)/You Never Give Me Your Money (Paul)/Sun King (John, Paul and George)/Mean Mr Mustard (Paul)/Polythene Pam (John)/She Came In Through the Bathroom Window (Paul)/Golden Slumbers (Paul)/Carry That Weight (John, Paul, George and Ringo)/The End (Paul)/Her Majesty (Paul).

'Abbey Road' is the last real album the Beatles ever made; and it was certainly the last time all four were co-operating together in the studio.

It was actually recorded *after* 'Let It Be' – but continuing problems with the latter delayed editing, then programming, and finally re-mixing; meanwhile, the issue of 'Abbey Road' took place.

The front sleeve photograph is sprinkled with 'clues', detectable only to bloodhound-like Beatleologists who interpreted (as the Beatles had undoubtedly guessed) many of the ominous symbols as indicating the recent Passing On of James Paul McCartney. All four Beatles are pictured in single file on a pedestrian crossing; Paul is out of step. He is also barefoot (a sign of mourning in Sicily), and his face is hidden from the camera's eye.

Other grim portents abound: if, as the ghouls insisted, McCartney had shuffled off this mortal coil some eighteen months before the issue of 'Abbey Road' – and his place had been taken by a mysterious android with, apparently, McCartney's full creative powers – then an

1969

March 21
John and Yoko slip between the sheets in the Amsterdam Hilton to campaign for peace. (*Below*)

April 22
Apple Press Office release: 'Beatle John Winston Lennon today changed his name to John Ono Lennon at a brief ceremony on the roof of the Beatles' Apple Company Head-quarters at 3 Savile Row, London, W1. The change of name was effected by Señor Bueno de Mesquita, Commissioner for Oaths.'

May 24–25
John and Yoko jet to Bahamas for Peace 'lie-in' but end up in Montreal.

July/August
'Abbey Road' sessions.

'John and Yoko? Some people think they're mad. But he's only being John!' Ringo Starr.

explanation is easily found for the unprecedented dominance which McCartney/Android exerts over this entire album. Prominent on the first side, McCartney practically carries the second side by himself – and this particular series of tracks still stands as one of the Beatles' supreme recorded achievements.

The album is largely a complicated collage of segued tracks whose apparent continuity probably owes more to skilful mixdown editing than to any definite 'concept' at the time of composition. But Lennon and McCartney had always composed in this way: some past songs had indeed been jointly written, but more often each would contribute a different section and these snippets would be welded together into a single piece (cf. 'A Day In The Life' from 'Sgt Pepper').

'Abbey Road' is certainly not unlike 'Pepper'. Both albums have the same glossy finish, noticeably lacking on all subsequent product apart from one or two singles. Both *appear* to follow a concept, though neither do in actuality and, in each case, the high standard of the master tape was arrived at by careful selection and juxtaposition, with effects added after-wards in the studio.

Lennon is strangely subdued once again, surfacing as a prominent vocalist only three times on 'Abbey Road' but with his unmistakable voice prominent on many of the backing layers. 'Come Together', the first song on the album, is his – and is one of the best of the set. Lennon's sardonic voice urges, through a barrage of free association, the exaltation of the simultane-ous orgasm.

Lennon himself thought 'Something', the next piece, 'the best song on the album'. George Harrison wrote 'Something' – and *his* well developed financial instincts must have been gladdened by the numerous royalties that flowed his way after this song was instantly seized on and re-recorded by many other artists. It proved, in fact, the most successful cut on the album, and was later issued (of course) as a single in both the UK and America. It's a soothing melody with highly decorative guitar and strong chord changes, easily as melodic as anything McCartney has written.

McCartney himself appears next with the rascally 'Maxwell's Silver Hammer', an effortless little tune about a psychotic medical student. McCartney's all-purpose children's TV-style voice makes Maxwell's homicidal progress sound almost banally normal. 'Oh! Darling' (the next track) is McCartney again, aping a Paul Anka two-straws-in-one-malted doo-wop lament. This slight sag in the texture and tension of 'Abbey Road' is given a further weight to contend with in the form of 'Octopus's Garden', a remake of 'Yellow Submarine' with further subnautical noises and little else to commend it. Ringo sings.

'I Want You – She's So Heavy' signals Lennon's return; it's a tortuous two-part piece which starts off like an agonised version of Mel Torme's 'Comin' Home Baby' and fades out amid the retreating footsteps of the Grim Reaper, as evoked by several instruments playing the same ominous riff in uncompromising unison.

George Harrison reportedly wrote 'Here Comes the Sun' in Eric Clapton's garden; if so, the solar orb was gleaming for him personally and not for Clapton, who was later to retire from playing altogether for a lengthy spell. This track was also heavily covered, and re-inforced Harrison's reputation as a mainstream Beatle composer. It featured, as did many of the tracks on 'Abbey Road', some exquisite three-part harmonies and an attractive com-bination of acoustic guitar and lead vocal.

A slower essay at the same craft, which displays, in parts, some really fine close harmonies, is the Hawaiian-sounding 'Because'. This segues sharply into the piano opening for McCart-ney's 'You Never Give Me Your Money' '*You only give me your funny paper*', he mourns as the piece builds and further vocal harmonies are layered on top. Graceful and very delicate, it drops abruptly into a boogie centre which leads away from the main theme into 'Sun King', which in turn immediately recalls 'Because' with its rich layerings of harmony (and nonsense Spanish).

At this point McCartney leaps to the fore. With one exception, all the remaining tracks on Side Two are his. The sequence in which they are welded produces some of the most accomplished – and surprising – music in Beatle repertoire.'Mean Mr Mustard'– who, if not a psychopath, is certainly extremely unsavoury – is once again passed off as a whimsical character, a sort of Elder Steptoe. Following very closely is Lennon's final track, 'Polythene Pam', his contribution to that gallery of weirdos who have detailed portraits in 'Abbey Road'. The closing three chords patter along for a while until they usher in McCartney's 'She Came In Through the Bathroom Window'. The 'significance of the symbolism' – *'She came in through the bathroom window/protected by a silver spoon'* – was another nail in McCartney's supposed coffin, but he survived long enough to reprise 'You Never Give Me Your Money' as 'Golden Slumbers'; a beautiful coda, 'The End', acts as a final decorative touch to the album (and particularly to his own final closing suite). Luckily, he had the necessary irreverence to puncture the effect thus created by adding a postscript. 'Her Majesty' lasts precisely twenty seconds.

The overall effect of 'Abbey Road' – especially when seen in its true scheduled context – is one of superb mockery, especially directed at the proliferating numbers of Beatleologists who were busily dissecting all Beatle LPs back to 'Rubber Soul' in a frantic search for Revelation. The music is some of the most polished and most memorable the group ever produced. In fact, McCartney was to have great difficulty in matching his own very considerable contributions for some years. The album dissatisfies because it is not perhaps their most honest record – but Beatle honesty veered perilously close to masochism on occasion and 'Abbey Roads' slickness is also its salvation.

'Cold Turkey' (John)/'Don't Worry Kyoko (Mummy's Only Looking For a Hand In the Snow') (Yoko)
Apple 1001. Produced: John Lennon and Yoko Ono
Released: October 24, 1969

'PLAY LOUD' demands the label in 24-point type, thus launching 'Cold Turkey's career with an excellent piece of advice. The personnel of the Plastic Ono Band had never been clearly defined – but in this case it boiled down to John Lennon (guitar and vocals), Eric Clapton (lead guitar), Klaus Voormann (bass) and Alan White (drums).

Due largely to Lennon's nerve-shredding vocal, it was the most powerful rocker that any solo Beatle had managed to produce to date – but it was its failure to raise higher than number thirteen in the charts which prompted Lennon to undertake one of his more majestic pieces of bad taste: miffed, he returned his MBE under plain brown wrapper, enclosing a note which simultaneously protested Britain's role in the Biafra War and his new single's disappointing chart action. This, in turn, prompted even more hostility from the Old Guard than his initial temerity in accepting the medal.

If the lyrics of 'Cold Turkey' were undeniably drug-orientated then the B-side – composed by Mrs Lennon – featured yet another instalment of the sufferings of the pair in their fraught attempts to win custody of Yoko Ono's child by a previous marriage, Kyoko.

'Something' (George)/'Come Together' (John)
Apple R 5814. Produced: George Martin
Released: October 31, 1969

One of the first acts of Allen Klein's management (of John, George and Ringo) was to lift this brace of 'Abbey Road' tracks for release as a single. There was some contention about doing so, supported by the single's failure to make the Number One slot – but 'Something' proved that, at long last, George Harrison was capable of producing a commercial, sensitive hit song in best Lennon/McCartney tradition.

The B-side, 'Come Together', Lennon's arch piece of proto-porn, is still part of his rare live repertoire and was recorded again (with Elephant's Memory) at the One-To-One Madison Square Garden concert. Neither the film or the album has yet been issued. Why?

1969

September 13
John and Yoko back in Toronto, this time with Eric Clapton, Klaus Voormann and Alan White for spectacular Rock 'n' Roll Revival Show.

September
The Lennons arrested at dawn and charged with possessing cannabis.

October
Russ Gibbs – Programme Co-ordinator for Station WKNR, Detroit, sparks off 'Paul is Dead' rumours. 'Abbey Road' LP sleeve scoured for hints that this might be so.

Top *John and Yoko in Canada with Timothy Leary (left) and Derek Taylor (middle).*

Above *Left to right: Klaus Voormann, Alan White, Yoko, John and Eric Clapton.*

83

1969

Below *Sleeve for the 'Wedding Album'*
Bottom *A subdued back sleeve for the
Plastic Ono Band.*

THE WEDDING ALBUM
Apple SAPCOR 11. Produced: John Lennon and Yoko Ono
Released: November 14, 1969
John and Yoko/Amsterdam

John Winston Lennon, 28 years, musician and composer, of Weybridge, Surrey, married Yoko Ono Cox, 36, artist, residing in Hanover Gate, W1, at Gibraltar on March 20, 1969. There were two witnesses . . . but the whole world witnessed the Lennons' honeymoon, which took the form of the notorious Amsterdam Hilton Bed-In later the same week.

The album which followed was intended to commemorate the wedding, if not the consummation. Unfortunately, the elaborate packaging schedule required eight months to complete, and the impact of these highly publicised nuptials was dissipated by the time 'The Wedding Album' reached the shops.

True to form, it was a disjointed, vaguely Warholesque concept in which the main action consisted of the names 'John' and 'Yoko' repeated in a variety of different textures for a whole LP side. Gets boring after the second 'John'.

Side Two is an *audio-verité* collection of sound-clippings recorded at their bedside.

The packaging included a replica of the marriage certificate, a postcard, some photographs, an album, a reproduction of a slice of the wedding cake and a book of press cuttings about the Lennon's antics. Most of these clippings are savage and intolerant – and extremely revealing about the reactions of the British race to exhibitionistic non-conformism.

'PLASTIC ONO BAND/LIVE PEACE IN TORONTO'
Apple CORE 2001. Produced: John Lennon and Yoko Ono
Released: December 12, 1969
Blue Suede Shoes/Money/Dizzy Miss Lizzy/Yer Blues/Cold Turkey/Give Peace a Chance/Don't Worry Kyoko/John, John

By this time Lennon was acting as if the Beatles split was official (which it was and it wasn't). So he went right ahead and, with the Plastic Ono Band – Eric Clapton (lead guitar), Klaus Voormann (bass), Alan White (drums) and Yoko – pointed himself in the general direction of Toronto. Refused by one major airline, they nonetheless bought tickets on a second, flew to Toronto, rehearsing in mid-flight, disembarked, drove direct to the Varsity Stadium, sank a couple of quick ones in the locker room – and cruised briskly on stage to obliterate 25,000 Canadians, plus several hundred visiting US citizens.

'Live Peace In Toronto' is a great album – if only for its spontaneity – and the choice of the material shows that, despite years of Beatles esoterica and peace junkettings, Lennon was still a devout rocker under his white suit and the accumulated layers of bagism and hair.

'We're goin' to do numbers we know', announced John, 'cause we've never played together before. But here goes and good luck'. After a quick count-in, he launched into a casual version of Carl Perkins' 'Blue Suede Shoes'. With that number Lennon took a deliberate step eight years into his past, and the following numbers on Side One, 'Money', 'Dizzy Miss Lizzy', 'Yer Blues', 'Cold Turkey' and 'Give Peace a Chance', added substantial weight to the no-nonsense nostalgia set which his band laid down that night with timeless aplomb and a good deal of dignity – contrasting favourably with the somewhat self-consious actions performed by Lennon in the previous two years.

Yoko, 'shrouded in a sheet' (as the *Toronto Telegram* disdainfully reported), squalled intermittently throughout the first side and sang, somewhat sparingly on the second; needless to say, it is the first side which sustains the album.

All these tracks succeed, especially the live version of 'Yer Blues' (from the 'White Album'). 'Cold Turkey', previewed here for the first time, makes it in spirit if not with the level of finesse captured on the studio release.

November 25
John returns his MBE 'with love' to
the Queen, in protest against
Britain's involvement in Biafra and
Vietnam — and against 'Cold Turkey'
slipping down the charts. In doing so,
Lennon stimulated even more
outrage than when he'd received the
award.

*'I share John's views about Britain's
involvement in the Nigerian war, but I
cannot agree that this is any way to
register a protest. If I'd known what
he wanted to do with it, I would
not have let him have his MBE.
This is all very much out of character
for John.'* John's Auntie Mimi
(Smith).

*'I am very upset that my Auntie Mimi
is upset. I will ring her to try and
explain why I handed the MBE back.
She doesn't understand half the
things I do. She hasn't yet got over
the fact that I started wearing side-
burns when I was 18.'* John Lennon.

December
George Harrison playing concerts
with US White-soulsters Delaney
and Bonnie.

December 15
Harrison and Delaney and Bonnie
jam with John and Yoko at 'War Is
Over (If You Want It)' Lyceum
concert.

'Genius is Pain.' John Lennon.

Right *One of the last pictures of the
Beatles playing as a group.*

'Instant Karma' (John)/'Who Has Seen the Wind' (Yoko)
Apple 1003. Produced: Phil Spector
Released: February 6, 1970

Written and recorded in one day, this snappy little rocker owes as much to the skilful production of Phil Spector as to the vitality of the overall performance – featuring John Lennon, George Harrison, Klaus Voormann and Alan White. In typical Spector fashion, the thick piano sound was contrived by no less than three separate instruments playing the same part. John was seated at one grand piano, George and Alan duetted on another, while Klaus Voormann played an electric keyboard.

The lead vocal features a recording technique that Lennon and Spector between them were to make unique and distinctive over the next four years. Basically, it depends upon heavy reverb; the effect is not unlike that achieved when singing in a small room filled with chromium fittings and tiled surfaces. The backing, so popular legend has it, was created by a parcel of shiftless liggers shanghaied especially for the occasion from a local trendy diskery.

Drummer Alan White excels.

The B-side would have made a marvellous soundtrack for the movie of Henry James' 'The Turn of the Screw', being a somewhat sinister ditty sung *à la Wunderkind* by Yoko Ono.

Incidentally, the promotion of this single lured Lennon back to British TV for his first live performance since 1965.

The version of 'Instant Karma' released in the UK incorporated a final mix ok'd by Lennon; the US version, however, Spector took on his own shoulders and it is noticeably less jagged.

'Let It Be' (Paul)/'You Know My Name' (John)
Apple R 5833. Produced: George Martin
Released: March 6, 1970

The increasingly complicated situation *vis-a-vis* Beatles/Plastic Ono Band/Phil Spector/ George Martin/Allen Klein/Lee and John Eastman/Apple/NEMS/Triumph Investment Trust/ Dick James/Northern Songs/ATV, produced a single with a diabolically confused web of interests involved.

Approximately, the story is that 'You Know My Name' was planned as the A-side with 'What's the New Mary Jane?' supporting, but contract troubles – an increasing and still-unsolved problem – forced the cancellation of this idea. But it is important to stress that this story is as recalled by only *some* of those involved: it is more than likely, with the chaotic state of Apple at the time, that nobody knew exactly what the new Beatles single was supposed to be until some nameless executive took the plunge and ordered the handouts printed. Next instalment sees 'Let It Be' – from the album of the movie of the prolonged fragmentation of the Beatles – chosen as A-side with 'Mary Jane' as the B. 'Mary Jane' didn't stay the pace, and the original selection 'You Know My Name', was reinstated on the single as support track. And after all that, the single only made the third slot. (In fact, the original selection would have been credited to the Plastic Ono Band . . . but we won't go into that).

Meanwhile, the actual single finally issued was yet another in the McCartney series of epilogue Beatle 45s. Like 'Hey Jude' in its hymnal quality, 'Let It Be' is a quasi-religious song with enough mock philosophy to satisfy a Jesuit. On the other hand, 'Mother Mary' *could* have been Paul's mother. The liturgical piano certainly sheds stained-glass radiance in all directions, and the celestial choir adds the right touch of sacerdotal schmaltz.

To add to the confusion, there were *two* issued versions of 'Let It Be'. The superior cut can be found on the album of the same name; George Harrison's guitar solo is discernibly more up-front and the brass deflates the pomposity. (Discarded takes of this song appear on bootlegs.)

The B-side, 'You Know My Name (Look Up the Number)' is a couldn't-care-less example of Disintegration Blues. It's funny. In places.

Above *Ringo's first solo album.*

Above right *Ringo rehearsing for a television show based on the album.*

SENTIMENTAL JOURNEY
Apple PCS 7101. Produced: George Martin
Released: April 3, 1970
Sentimental Journey/Night and Day/Whispering Grass (Don't Tell the Trees)/Bye Bye Blackbird/I'm a Fool To Care/Stardust/Blue, Turning Grey Over You/Love Is a Many Splendoured Thing/Dream/You Always Hurt the One You Love/Have I Told You Lately I Love You/Let the Rest Of the World Go By.

The week after Ringo's first solo album was issued, Paul McCartney trumpeted his decision to leave the Beatles. Could it possibly have been due to the staggeringly poor quality of this most embarrassing (to date) of all Beatles solo excursions?

'I did it for me Mum', apologised Ringo, when faced with raised eyebrows from his peer group. It's to be hoped that Mrs Starkey applauded his selections, because in the eyes of most others this was a gawky, badly sung, overly sentimental selection of moribund mambos. All are dispensable.

He was to do a little better next time.

April 10
'Beatles to Break Up' stories headline world's press following McCartney's Declaration of Independence.

April 27
Lennon's lithos declared 'unlikely to deprave or corrupt' by legal experts and handed back.

July 31
Cynthia Lennon marries Roberto Bassanini.

December 30
Paul McCartney sues remaining three Beatles; shows *prima facie* case.

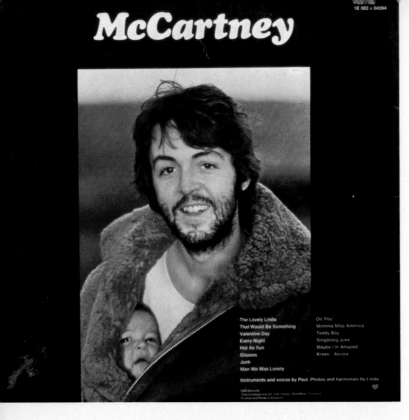

Paul pictured with his baby on the back of the album sleeve.

McCARTNEY
Apple PCS 7102. Produced: Paul McCartney
Released: April 17, 1970
The Lovely Linda/That Would Be Something/Valentine Day/Every Night/Hot As Sun/ Glasses/Junk/Man We Was Lonely/Oo You/Momma Miss America/Teddy Boy/Singalong Junk/Maybe I'm Amazed/Kreen-Akrore

Because McCartney was in very bad odour – with his fellow Beatles, with Klein, and with a public infuriated by his decision to quit – this album landed on the receiving end of much hostility. An additional complication lay in the fact that 'McCartney' and the next 'official' Beatle LP, 'Let It Be', were issued practically simultaneously.

McCartney later said: 'There was some hassle at the time. We were arguing over who had mentioned a release date first. It was all a bit petty; I'd pegged a release date and then "Let It Be" was scheduled near it. I saw it as victimisation but now I'm sure it wasn't.'

Petty or not, things were so unpleasant between the Beatles that when John and George sent Ringo round as ambassador to sort out the mess, an irate Paul indicated the vulnerability of the Nose, threatened to 'finish him off' and threw him out of the house.

And was it all really worth it? This album was conspicuously hand-made (with a Studer four-track and one microphone) and this makeshift quality was resented by those acclimatised to super-sophisticated Beatle product. It was also extremely hastily made, and the very unpretentious qualities which McCartney tried to emphasise were badly misconstrued as ineptitude.

Hindsight displays its charms.

McCartney himself doesn't claim much for this album – and yet it contains one truly superb song, 'Maybe I'm Amazed'; and the others are certainly inoffensive. In any event, compared with John and Yoko's 'Wedding Album', it displayed a lot more care and a great deal less posturing.

LET IT BE
Apple PCS 7096. Produced: George Martin, Glyn Johns and Phil Spector
Released: May 8, 1970
Two Of Us (John and Paul)/Dig a Pony (John)/Across the Universe (John)/I Me Mine (George)/ Dig It (John)/Let It Be (Paul)/Maggie Mae (John)/I've Got a Feeling (Paul)/One After 909 (John and Paul)/The Long and Winding Road (Paul)/For You Blue (George)/Get Back (Paul)

The very fact of there being no less than *three* separate production credits on this album underscores the ill-starred nature of this operation. Between the date of the original recording session and the date of issue lay fifteen months of squabbling, apathy, disowning, re-mixing and civil litigation.

'If the Beatles soundtrack album "Let It Be" is to be their last then it will stand as a cheapskate epitaph, a cardboard tombstone, a sad and tatty end to a musical fusion which wiped clean and drew again the face of pop music.' Alan Smith – *New Musical Express.*

Left *Three stills from the film* Let It Be.

Opposite page *And the album sleeve.*

'Let It Be' can be seen now as a prophetic title. After the film, this is just about what they did. In spite of some fine moments, notably the rooftop session (top), the film comes across as a documentary of a disintegrating group rather than a live and flourishing one. The venture was about a year too late.

91

THE SOLO YEARS

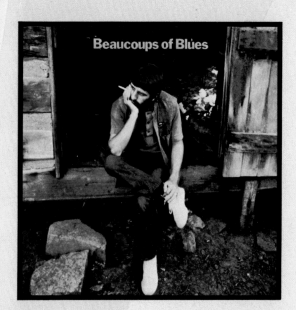

BEAUCOUPS OF BLUES
Apple PAS 10002. Produced: Pete Drake
Released: September 25, 1970
Beaucoups Of Blues/Love Don't Last Long/Fastest Growing Heartache In the West/Without Her/Woman Of the Night/I'd Be Talking All the Time/$15 Draw/Wine, Women and Loud Happy Songs/I Wouldn't Have You Any Other Way/Loser's Lounge/Waiting/Silent Homecoming

Ringo's second solo album – and substantially better than his first. His ethnic Liverpool yearnings reached full nostalgic flower on this charmingly insubstantial selection of contemporary country-and-western numbers.

Despite the entire Beatle career, Ringo showed – with all his solo work – that the exoticism of 'Pepper' and 'Magical Mystery Tour' had exerted no lasting influence over him.

Recorded in Nashville with the best of the local musicians available on the session, it was a swift, professional job and reportedly took less than a week to make. There is apparently a sizeable residue of unused tracks, which may one day make a further album.

Note: in the States, 'Beaucoups of Blues' was released as a single with a song called 'Coochy Coo' which never appeared in England.

ALL THINGS MUST PASS
Apple STCH 639. Produced: George Harrison and Phil Spector
Released: November 27, 1970
I'd Have You Any Time/My Sweet Lord/Wah-Wah/Isn't It a Pity – Version One/What Is Life/If Not For You/Behind That Locked Door/Let It Down/Run Of the Mill/Beware Of Darkness/Apple Scruffs/Ballad Of Sir Frankie Crisp (Let It Roll)/Awaiting On You All/All Things Must Pass/I Dig Love/Art Of Dying/Isn't It a Pity – Version Two/Hear Me Lord/Out Of the Blue/It's Johnny's Birthday/Plug Me In/I Remember Jeep/Thanks For the Pepperoni

'All Things Must Pass' was issued in time to reap the Christmas sale – which the Beatles had been failing to do for several years. Strictly speaking, it was a double album, the third side being a live jam session involving minimal expense. Nonetheless, the asking price was in excess of five pounds, which many considered expensive for the times.

It has not worn well – due, above all, to the homogeneity of the production and the lugubrious nature of Harrison's composing. The most controversial track, 'My Sweet Lord', stimulated angry comparisons with the Chiffons' 'He's So Fine' and also betrayed the portentous nature of some of George's more religious-inspired material.

Although none of the songs are as original as 'Something', 'Here Come the Sun' – or even 'If I Needed Someone' (on the 'Rubber Soul' LP) – the album sold in great quantities. A strong hook was the phantom presence of Bob Dylan: Harrison co-wrote 'I'd Have You Any Time' with the Maestro, and 'If Not For You' is an actual Dylan original. Star guitarist Eric Clapton appears on 'Apple Jam', while the main session features Klaus Voormann, Ringo, Alan White, Billy Preston, Ginger Baker, Gary Brooker (vocalist and pianist with

Top *Ringo's second solo album.*
Above *And George's third.*

92

Procol Harum) plus all 'Derek's' Dominos.

The songs, as has been mentioned, seem somewhat weak in these latter days. Spector's burying techniques tended to cover what original melody existed in the first place – but perhaps it was the sheer scale of the project which proved too much for Harrison's powers of continuous creativity. His somewhat solemn nature also pervades most of the album . . . to its detriment. Nonetheless, it was made with care – and on schedule – and can, from that point of view, be considered a successful record.

JOHN LENNON/PLASTIC ONO BAND
Apple PCS 7124. Produced: John Lennon, Yoko Ono and Phil Spector
Released: December 11, 1970
Mother/Hold On John/I Found Out/Working Class Hero/Isolation/Remember/Love/Well Well Well/Look At Me/God/My Mummy's Dead

A majestic album and, with Paul McCartney's 'Band On the Run' (issued three years later), one of the two best-ever Beatle solo LPs.

Lennon's solo work had, until now, taken the form of collaborations with wife Yoko which reflected more of her influences than of his. But two years in the wilderness had produced a strong undercurrent of feeling in Lennon which could not be satisfied by lying on art-gallery floors inside large paper bags. His own splintered childhood and his recent discovery of primal scream therapy techniques encouraged him to use the LP medium as confessional, thereby laying some of the ghosts which had haunted him since early adolescence. The result is a remarkable and often moving album, almost brutally honest, and which, though obsessed with personal pain, was a complete artistic statement of great courage and typical candour.

Indeed, so many and so horrendous were the chances taken by Lennon on this LP that, with any lesser talent, the result could have been disastrous. In the word of a review of the time, he placed his balls defiantly on the line; out of sheer respect, the train ground to a halt.

A quick scan of the track titles reveals much of the subject matter: his rejection by the community as an adolescent; his rejection by the world (and his fellow-Beatles) in recent months; his loss of his mother in childhood – nothing is spared the listener, and the fact that such harrowing material succeeds artistically without falling into the trap of sentiment is entirely due to Lennon's natural feeling for economy and sparseness which preclude all forms of conventional musical sentimentality.

Dry-eyed, he sings of his mother, Julia ('Mother', 'My Mummy's Dead'); of painful growing-up and equally painful later rejection ('Working Class Hero'); of sham idolatry as personally experienced ('I Found Out', 'Isolation', 'God') – and, occasionally, of discovery and hope for the future ('Hold On John', 'Love', 'Look At Me').

The particularly brutal – though utterly appropriate – lyrics to 'Working Class Hero' caused predictable problems for Lennon: the word fuck is used twice, though the dramatic requirements more than justify it. In Britain, the BBC banned the track (they could hardly do anything else), but this only added pungency to the lyric's meaning.

Generally speaking, the album reeks of disillusion. Nonetheless, it was widely hailed as a *bona fide* artistic statement, and many welcomed Lennon's return to active recording. The LP is especially notable for the first appearance of the later well-known 'bathroom' effect on Lennon's vocal, which he was to retain through his next three solo LPs. The fullness of the instrumental was remarkable considering the sparseness of the line-up: Lennon, guitars, piano; Klaus Voormann, bass; Ringo Starr, drums. (Occasional keyboard parts were played by Billy Preston and Phil Spector himself.)

This period of Lennon's creativity has recently been harshly parodied – probably because of the excess of agony to be found in the songs. All the same, it was the most worthwhile Beatle LP since 'Abbey Road' and was not to be equalled by any other until late 1973.

Top *A pastoral sleeve for John and Yoko's latest album.*

Above *John as 'Working Class Hero'.*

93

January 19
Beatles in court: 'Paul behaved like a spoilt child' says Ringo under oath.

March 3
South African Radio lifts five-year ban.

March 12
Receiver appointed in Beatles litigation.

March 19
John, George and Ringo appeal against appointment of Receiver.

June 20
Mavis Smith leaves Apple Press Office. One minute's silence.

'Paul's criticisms of Allen Klein may reflect his dislike of the man, but I don't think they are fair. Klein is certainly forceful to an extreme but he does get results. He didn't sow discord between us.' John Lennon.

'To get a peaceful life I always let Paul have his own way, even when it meant that my songs weren't recorded. But I was having to record Paul's songs and put up with him telling me how to play my own guitar.' George Harrison.

'The Beatles have not been prejudiced by my dealings. They have greatly benefitted. The assets of the Beatles partnership are in no way in jeopardy.' Allen Klein.

'People were robbing us and living off us to the tune of ... 18 or 20 thousand pounds a week was rolling out of Apple and nobody was doing anything about it.' John Lennon.

The Ono-Lennons in the apparel of fully fledged politicos. These were the photographs used on the sleeve of 'Power To the People'.

'My Sweet Lord'/'What Is Life'
Apple R 5884. Produced: George Harrison and Phil Spector
Released: January 15, 1971

From the enormously successful 'All Things Must Pass' package, Apple lifted this reverent single to provide extra gravy. Like the LP it was also enormously successful – topping almost every chart in the world – but ran into deep trouble with the writers and publishers of 'He's So Fine', a perennial golden oldie originally recorded by the Chiffons in 1963. The differences between the two songs are minimal.

'Another Day'/'Oh Woman, Oh Why'
Apple R 5889. Produced: Paul and Linda McCartney
Released: February 26, 1971

Paul, who had been falling somewhat behind in the solo release stakes, emerged with his first solo single early in 1971. Naturally, the lovely Linda also appears; the combined effect is distastefully bourgeois, especially after Lennon's recent confessional – the sheer triteness of this single came across as disappointingly mediocre. Would have made a superb TV commercial for underarm charm.

'Power To the People'/'Open Your Box'
Apple R 5892. Produced: John Lennon, Yoko Ono and Phil Spector
Released: March 6, 1971

Enter the Ono-Lennons decked out in Japanese riot gear . . . and farewell, temporarily, to the peace-loving Ono-Lennons of Amsterdam and Toronto. Gentle urgings gave way to rabble-rousing (with the Ono-Lennons portrayed in the publicity pictures with up-raised clenched fists).

Unfortunately, the dreadful curse of the brainless militant was to linger for some time, but in 1971 it had not reached its full ferocious climax, and 'Power To the People' still boils down to a comparatively harmless – and reasonably justified – plea for a square deal for the underprivileged.

The B-side was banned in America, being construed as an invocation to promiscuity.

'It Don't Come Easy'/'Early 1970'
Apple R 5898. Produced: George Harrison
Released: April 2, 1971

And Ringo, ironically enough, did much better with *his* first single, doubtless because his confidence had been reinforced by the relative success of 'Beaucoups Of Blues' (his second album).

Easy to assimilate, catchy, and charmingly inane, it was extensively plugged and ended up in the Top Five.

RAM
Apple PAS 10003. Produced: Paul and Linda McCartney
Released: May 21, 1971
Too Many People/3 Legs/Ram On/Dear Boy/Uncle Albert – Admiral Halsey/Smile Away/ Heart Of the Country/Monkberry Moon Delight/Eat At Home/Long Haired Lady/Ram On/ The Back Seat Of My Car

Of all the Beatles, it was probably Paul McCartney who was most on the defensive during the 1971–72 period. And it's not difficult to guess the reason why: as prime contender for the title Breaker-Up-Of-The-Beatles, he was virtually estranged from the other three and, unlike John, had not married a lady with any particular solo talent; Linda's ability lay – and still lies – in providing a moral pillow for her man.

'Ram' reflects this one-sided situation. It would be naive to have expected the McCartneys to produce anything other than a fairly mediocre record. And so it is. Only five tracks ('Uncle Albert', 'Smile Away', 'Heart Of the Country', 'Monkberry Moon Delight' and the excellent 'Back Seat Of My Car') are really still worthy of investigation.

'Suburban Pop 'n' Roll', sneered the critics – but it was neither good pop (being too contrived) nor good rock (being too saccharine). It was sta-prest ready-to-wear music, to be listened to in a lounge with plaster ducks on the wall, and it positively reeked of cosy domestica – the kind of environment which stifles all creativity.

But this, by all accounts, was deliberate. Paul's long-drawn-out yearnings for cucumber sandwiches at the local Rotary Club and a family of his own were further emphasised by the cover photo, taken on his Scottish farm, showing the genial Beatle, gumbooted, proudly fondling a ram. Grisly though this was, McCartney was to sink lower before rescuing his credibility late in 1973. (*Sleeve photo on following page.*)

THE EARLY YEARS
Contour 2870111. Produced: Bert Kaempfert
Released: June 1971
Ain't She Sweet (John)/Cry For a Shadow (instrumental)/Let's Dance*/My Bonnie/Take Out Some Insurance On Me Baby**/What'd I Say*/Sweet Georgia Brown**/The Saints**/ Ruby Baby*/Why Can't You Love Me Again**/Nobody's Child**/Ya-Ya***
* Tony Sheridan – vocal; Beat Brothers – backing
** Tony Sheridan – vocal; Beatles – backing

Tony Sheridan was, at the time this LP was made (spring 1961), the leader of the Star Band, house outfit of the famous Hamburg Star Club. These sessions represent Bert Kämpfert's attempt to make Sheridan into a solo artist – a position the immensely talented but notoriously disorganised singer/guitarist richly deserved.

Above *Ringo as Frank Zappa in the latter's film, 200. Zappa himself stands behind Ringo.*

Right *An attempt to boost Tony Sheridan. The record was originally made in 1961, and re-released ten years later.*

Above *The press conference following the announcement of the Bangla Desh concert. Allen Klein sits on George's right.*

Above right *Paul cuts a rural figure on the 'Ram' sleeve, a perfect target for John's bitter wit (see opposite page).*

July 27
George announces the concert for Bangla Desh.

July 31
Two concerts to help relieve war-torn Bangla Desh are held at New York's Madison Square Garden, featuring George, Ringo, Dylan, Eric Clapton, Ravi Shankar, Leon Russell and Billy Preston.

August 3
Paul announces formation of Wings.

December 11
John and Yoko participate in John Sinclair Ann Arbor Benefit.

'Bangla Desh'/'Deep Blue'
Apple R 5912. Produced: George Harrison and Phil Spector
Released: August 7, 1971

With his close associations with the sub-continent, George took the Bangla Desh catastrophe very seriously indeed. The first of the public gestures he made (with the laudable aim of bringing aid to the homeless and hungry of that unfortunate land) was the issue of this single, proceeds from which went towards that end. The second – and more spectacular – effort in this field was the mammoth all-star concert he organised in New York the following month.

With such worthy objectives, it's a shame the single was as poor as it turned out to be. The backing thunders along competently enough, but Harrison's weedy vocal and uncertain pitching are not sufficient in themselves to carry a vocal line which, because of the tortuous intervals, needs to be clearly defined.

'Bangla Desh' did moderately well and thus performed the service for which it was specifically intended.

'The Back Seat Of My Car'/'Heart Of the Country'
Apple R 5914. Produced: Paul and Linda McCartney
Released: August 14, 1971

From 'Ram', the McCartneys chose what was easily the best song of the collection to be their next single. Like the album, it features assistance from musicians Dave Spinoza and Hugh McCracken (guitars) and Denny Seiwell (drums), and depends largely on their expertise in order to fulfil its considerable musical ambitions. It was the closest thing to a 'constructed' song that McCartney had produced since 'Abbey Road' – and is good enough to be judged on that level, though it had little success.

IMAGINE
Apple PAS 10004. Produced: John Lennon, Yoko Ono and Phil Spector
Released: October 2, 1971
Imagine/Crippled Inside/Jealous Guy/It's So Hard/I Don't Want To Be a Soldier/Give Me Some Truth/Oh My Love/How Do You Sleep?/How?/Oh Yoko!

'Imagine', extremely well received at the time of issue, still stands as a classic of its kind and the most positive recorded statement Lennon has yet managed to make without the collaboration of Paul McCartney – though certain aspects of its premise have undergone some reassessment.

Pain, the stock-in-trade of the archetypal singer/song writer – and featured in pallid technicolour by Lennon himself on his earlier album – found itself subtly muted in favour of melody, polish, and a surprising sense of optimism. This was his White Period. He wore white, played a white piano, laundered his thoughts to breath-taking freshness (with one curious exception) and breathed white fumes in the white room of his white house at Ascot.

Because of the blanched nature of the publicity surrounding 'Imagine', the album itself seems full of colour. Lennon runs a full gamut of emotions, from 1970 agony to 1971 ecstasy with a sideswipe at arch-litigant Paul McCartney thrown in for good measure and malicious intent. 'How Do You Sleep?' is the most extraordinary song on the entire album. It is a vitriolic open letter, full of nasty insinuations and contemptuous insults. George Harrison's presence on this particular track almost makes it a *sub-judice* statement (McCartney's lawsuit was currently drawing to a finale). Just in case anyone missed the point, the album package contained a postcard-sized photograph of Lennon fondling a pig in the style of McCartney's 'Ram' album cover.

All the more surprising then, that the majority of the remaining nine tracks display a gentleness and sensitivity far removed from the crude personal level of 'How Do You Sleep'. In fact, Lennon's rediscovery of melody – and it is nearly *all* melodic music that we encounter on this album – is gratifying in view of his almost total abandonment of this quality, both before and since. But for 'How Do You Sleep?' one would almost declare 'Imagine' a loving album. Perhaps the most lyrical tracks are 'Jealous Guy' and the title track itself. 'Oh My Love' and 'Oh Yoko!' are also tender little tunes. There is some of the 'Plastic Ono Band' period self-flagellation ('Crippled Inside', 'I Don't Want To Be a Soldier' and 'Give Me Some Truth') and, of course, the unique 'How Do You Sleep?'.

Phil Spector's bronco talent has never been too much for Lennon to handle: on this album the short-delay reverb on the vocal tracks, characteristic of the Lennon/Spector partnership, crystalised into a stylistic asset. This particular vocal sound was also to characterise Lennon's next two LPs but neither were as artistically or commercially successful as 'Imagine'.

WILD LIFE
Apple PCS 7142. Produced: Paul and Linda McCartney
Released: November 15, 1971
Mumbo/Bip Bop/Love Is Strange/Wild Life/Some People Never Know/I Am Your Singer/Tomorrow/Dear Friend

The McCartney's musical credibility plummetted sharply on the release of this album. 'Wild Life' was rushed, defensive, badly timed and over-publicised.

For some time the McCartneys had threatened to form a permanent road band and, to their credit, this was achieved in late 1971; US drummer Denny Seiwell and ex-Moody Blues guitarist/singer Denny Laine joined Paul and Linda: the combination was dubbed Wings.

To be brief (but unkind) it is a pretty futile exercise, and represents McCartney's composing abilities at an absolute nadir just when he needed a little respect. The point is further emphasised by the saddening fact that the only semi-acceptable track, 'Love Is Strange', was a reggae re-run of the old Mickey and Sylvia hit. (*Sleeve photo on following page.*)

Top *Lennon's 'Imagine', featuring some superb music and a vitriolic attack on Paul. The album's give-away photograph (above) is such an obvious take-off of the 'Ram' sleeve that no one could possibly miss the point.*

97

Top *George and Bob Dylan at the concert for Bangla Desh.*

Above *Sleeve for Wings' 'Wild Life'.*

Right *The Wings line-up. Left to right: Henry McCullough, Paul, Linda, Denny Seiwell, Denny Laine.*

THE CONCERT FOR BANGLA DESH

Apple STCX 3385. Produced: George Harrison and Phil Spector
Released: January 8, 1972
George Harrison, Ravi Shankar Introduction/Bangla Dhun (Ravi Shankar)/Wah-Wah (George)/My Sweet Lord (George)/Awaiting On You All (George)/That's The Way God Planned It (Billy Preston)/It Don't Come Easy (Ringo Starr)/Beware Of Darkness (George)/While My Guitar Gently Weeps (George)/Jumping Jack Flash (Leon Russell)/Youngblood (Leon Russell)/Here Comes The Sun (George)/A Hard Rain's Gonna Fall (Bob Dylan)/It Takes a Lot To Laugh It Takes a Train To Cry (Bob Dylan)/Blowin' In the Wind (Bob Dylan)/Mr Tambourine Man (Bob Dylan)/Just Like a Woman (Bob Dylan)/Something (George Harrison)/Bangla Desh (George Harrison)

Probably the greatest indoor rock 'n' roll event ever held was the Concert for Bangla Desh, organised by George Harrison, which took place on August 1, 1971, at New York's Madison Square Garden.

The almost unparalleled cast included Harrison himself, Bob Dylan, Eric Clapton, Ringo Starr, Billy Preston, Leon Russell, Ravi Shankar, Klaus Voormann, Jim Keltner and Carl Radle – plus many other luminaries. To assemble such an awesome grouping was a considerable feat in itself; Lennon and McCartney, reportedly invited, declined – but the welcome surprise of Bob Dylan's unbilled appearance, bringing a cry of delight from the throats of 20,000 concertgoers, easily compensated.

No less an achievement was the immaculate standard of rehearsal attained in a very short time under siege conditions. The six sides which total this set are remarkable, not only for the excellence of the recording, but for the faultless musicianship throughout.

Harrison's own contributions are retreads from his best-selling 'All Things Must Pass' album plus a few from 'Abbey Road' and 'The White Album'.

Ravi Shankar, who co-organised the event with Harrison, opens the proceedings in sombre fashion with a strict injunction to the audience to remember the reasons for the concert; he then completes the rest of Side One, assisted by his musicians, with an expert series of pieces composed especially for the occasion. Side Two is mainly Harrison. Billy Preston closes the volume with his good-time religious hit 'That's the Way God Planned It'. Ringo opens the third side with 'It Don't Come Easy' and then hands the spot-light back to Harrison with 'Beware Of Darkness' and 'While My Guitar Gently Weeps' (which features Eric Clapton on guitar). Oklahoma session-opportunist Leon Russell takes care of most of the fourth segment in typical brash manner with a polished medley: the Stones' 'Jumping Jack Flash' and the Coasters' 'Youngblood'. Then Apple apprentices Badfinger join Harrison on stage for the acoustic 'Here Comes the Sun'.

The album's vast cost (£5.50) was easily justified by the superb fifth side alone. 'Like to bring on a friend of us all – Mr Bob Dylan', announces Harrison with almost unbelievable laconicism. And Dylan emerged on stage before the astounded eyes of the assembled multitude to deliver five of his classic songs with great professionalism and a fine eye for the mood of the crowd. It is almost as an anti-climax that the album concludes with Harrison's 'Something' and – presumably to drive the real point of the concert home – a fairly tepid rendering of his 'Bangla Desh' single.

Unfortunately for Harrison's good intentions, obtaining the necessary clearances from the various record companies involved (notably CBS) proved more difficult than originally envisaged. In fact, in the five month's interim between concert and album, bootlegs actually began to appear on the market. Luckily, most differences were resolved by January, and the LP – which had, by now, exceeded its original 'expenses-only' premise – went on sale to the ultimate benefit of the destitute Bengalis for whom the whole project was intended. Further delays ensued before threatened civil action finally caused the proceeds to head in an easterly direction – a slightly sordid end to an overwhelmingly generous gesture and a superb concert. *(Sleeve photo on following page.)*

1972

January
World première of Ringo's new movie *Blind Man*.

February 8
Beatles Fan Club liquidates shop.

February 9
Wings make first (unannounced) appearance at Nottingham as part of hit-n-run college tour tactics.

March 18
Enter Ringo Starr film-maker, with camera trained on pop star Marc Bolan at London's Wembley Pool.

Ringo with Marc Bolan in Born To Boogie.

99

John and Yoko playing with Elephant's Memory for a US television broadcast.

May 21
BBC Radio One commence *The Beatles Story* serial.

July 9
Wings kick off extensive European junket at Château Fallon, France.

August
Ringo starts work on another new movie, *The Son of Dracula*.

August 10
The McCartneys charged with drug possession by Swedish authorities.

August 30
John and Yoko – plus Elephant's Memory and all-star supporting bill – stage two charity shows at Madison Square Garden, New York, in aid of the 'One-to-One' fund for handicapped children.

September 20
Zealous Scottish police raid McCartney's Campbelltown farm with the same results as their

'Give Ireland Back To the Irish'/'Give Ireland Back To the Irish (version)'
Apple R 5936. Produced: Paul and Linda McCartney
Released: February 19, 1972
McCartney, usually apolitical, surprised many when he issued this strongly-worded single shortly after Bloody Sunday, when paratroopers shot and killed thirteen during a Northern Ireland demonstration. Though the sentiments contained in the song seem – and seemed at the time – naive, then the BBC, quoting its charter, took 'Give Ireland Back To the Irish' seriously enough to feel justified in imposing an outright ban on airtime for the single.

'Back Off Boogaloo'*/'Blindman'*
Apple 5944. Produced: *George Harrison; *Ringo Starr and Klaus Voormann
Released: March 18, 1972

One of the curiosities of the post-split Beatles is that Ringo Starr's singles have done consistently better than those of his former colleagues – with the possible exception of George Harrison. His ear for commercial music rapidly became more acute, resulting in at least three excellent tunes, all of which did well in the charts . . . without ever establishing Ringo as a major force.
 'Back Off Boogaloo' was no exception, reaching a creditable second slot. Musically, it strongly reflects Ringo's close relationship at the time with then up-and-coming British pop idol Marc Bolan. Indeed, Ringo directed the movie 'Born To Boogie' which glorifies Bolan's 1972–73 British successes.

'Mary Had a Little Lamb'/'Little Woman Love'
Apple R 5949. Produced: Paul and Linda McCartney
Released: May 6, 1972

Whatever the true reasons for this deplorable single may be, it is difficult not to draw the conclusion that McCartney, piqued at the banning of his 'Give Ireland Back To the Irish' single, deliberately recorded nursery rhyme lyrics as a gesture of contempt towards the censors in question.
 As always with McCartney, the degree of effort put into a polished final performance is commendable. In essence a slow calypso with pleasant chord-changes and attractive banjo/guitar rhythm, it could have provided a backdrop for a subdued and catchy album track. In fact, its success was by no means inadequate: it reached the sixth position in the British

Above *'The Concert For Bangla Desh'* LP *sleeve.*

Above right *George performs with passion at the Bangla Desh concert.*

Below right *Dramatic lighting for Paul, on tour again.*

'Suddenly you're 30 and there's still so much more to do.' John Lennon.

'Funnily enough, I tend to remember the times before the Beatles happened — Hamburg and the Cavern. In those days we weren't just doing an entertainment thing or whatever the hell it was we were supposed to be. That's when we played music.' John Lennon.

'Filming Marc Bolan at Wembley was a nostalgic experience for me.' Ringo Starr.

'To me, the Beatles Story is a bit like an obituary.' Paul McCartney.

'Before we settled on the name Wings, we were nearly the Dazzlers — big sequinned jackets.' Paul McCartney.

'Klein will get his in the end.' Linda McCartney.

Artistically, it represents the lowest point the harassed and besieged McCartney was to reach. His music steadily improved from this point onwards – as his self-confidence began to return.

SOME TIME IN NEW YORK CITY
Apple PCSP 716. Produced: John Lennon, Yoko Ono and Phil Spector
Released: September 16, 1972
Side One* Woman Is the Nigger Of the World (John)/Sisters O Sisters (Yoko)/Attica State (John)/Born In a Prison (Yoko)/New York City (John)
Side Two* Sunday Bloody Sunday (John)/The Luck Of the Irish (John)/John Sinclair (John)/Angela (John)/We're All Water (Yoko)
Side Three** Cold Turkey (John)/Don't Worry Kyoko (Yoko)
Side Four*** Well (Baby Please Don't Go) (John)/Jamrag (John and Yoko)/Scumbag (John and Yoko)/Aii (Yoko)
* Plus Elephant's Memory with the Invisible Strings
** Plastic Ono Band only
*** Plastic Ono Band plus Frank Zappa and the Mothers of Invention.

The care and attention lavished on this double-album set promised great things – it was obviously intended to match the scale and quality (and commercial success) of George Harrison's 'All Things Must Pass'. But if Harrison's album suffered from over-seriousness and more than its fair share of tedium, then the Ono-Lennons' LP set stands condemned of mindless overkill, cheap rhetoric and a dismaying lack of proportion. Its only real virtues – spontaneity and, in some places, first-class musicianship – did not compensate for the appallingly bad lyrics and clichéd political phraseology.

There is some excuse: Lennon was living in a New York radical-chic ghetto, surrounded by committed political figures and a fair percentage of the usual big-city cultural vampires.

Below *'Some Time in New York City'* LP *sleeve.*

Below right *John, Yoko and Phil Spector (seated on John's right) with Elephant's Memory.*

Having deliberately rejected world leadership *as a Beatle*, Lennon allowed himself to be manipulated *as John Lennon*, ex-Beatle; his prestige was tacked on to many causes, some clearly defined, others less so. With typical sense of commitment, Lennon plumped for both, in equal measure. The album comes from that period and reads (for it is primarily a 'lyrics' album) like a vague political manifesto for every radical grievance then fashionable.

All of which detracts from the music, provided by a pool of extremely capable musicians – in particular the New York outfit Elephant's Memory, led by saxist Stan Bronstein. The combination of Spector's production, Bronstein's horn and the thunder of Lennon's voice (for his rock 'n' roll skills have *never* deserted him) is quite awesome at times: it is only when one listens to the words – traditionally one of the chief rewards of Beatle music – that a sense of disappointment (even outrage) pervades.

This is not to be taken to mean that the authors necessarily disagree with the sentiments expressed. Among the issues nobly confronted with verbal bazookas are: Northern Ireland; the Attica State Prison shootings; the imprisonment of radicals Angela Davis and John Sinclair; more Ireland; Women's Liberation; and more Ireland.

The album was received with great hostility in England (understandably) and with lukewarm semi-enthusiasm in the USA, where it had moderate-to-good chart success, probably based more on the Lennon name than on the lyrics contained in the songs. Even the radicals in Britain, however, regarded it as crass rubbish – coming from someone living comfortably in New York, the revolutionary sentiments could hardly be taken in any other light. Lennon's prestige plummetted to a record low: a nation who had (as they saw it) made him what he was found it difficult to stand calmly by while Lennon fervently labelled all 54 million as guilty of genocide and worse crimes. 'Sometime In New York City' was undoubtedly Lennon's worst mistake – and, at the time of writing, he has yet fully to recover from it.

Side Three, less shrill, features the Plastic Ono Band and material from the Lennons' 'War-is-over-if-you-want-it' period, recorded at the London Lyceum in 1969. Playing on the session are: Eric Clapton, George Harrison (guitars); Billy Preston, Nicky Hopkins (keyboards); Klaus Voormann (bass); Jim Gordon, Alan White and Keith Moon (drums); Bobby Keyes (sax) plus the entire Delaney Bonnie & Friends band. For all that, it is fairly cacophonous.

'Happy Xmas (War Is Over)'/'Listen, the Snow Is Falling'
Apple R 5970. Produced: John Lennon, Yoko Ono and Phil Spector
Released: November 25, 1972

As can be told by its peaceful nature (in stark contrast to the vitriolic 'Some Time In New York City' LP) this single dates from Lennon's white-suited, pacifistic period. It took nearly a year, owing to publishing intrigues, to obtain a British release.

'Hi Hi Hi'/'C Moon'
Apple R 5973. Produced: Paul and Linda McCartney
Released: December 2, 1972

McCartney's second song to be banned by the BBC, this time for lyrics 'which might be taken to endorse the use of drugs'. We will forbear from comment upon this decision, confining our critique to 'this is quite good', and 'not bad at all'. Certainly, one finds the battered McCartneys clambering manfully back on to their gumbooted feet and into public esteem with a catchy, inoffensive little rocker.

Actually, the B-side, 'C Moon', was infinitely superior and showed that McCartney had successfully mastered the reggae stumble. Probably his best individual song since 'Maybe I'm Amazed' from the 'McCartney' album. The public certainly liked it, putting it into third position on the charts.

Top *The much-beleagured Paul rehearsing in Montreux.*

Above *The Ono-Lennons in government surplus gear.*

103

1973

February
Ringo steps back fifteen years for co-starring (and acclaimed) role in British movie *That'll Be The Day*.

Right Director Claude Whatham (left) chats with Ringo and David Essex about a scene in That'll Be the Day.
Below and bottom Stills from the same film. Ringo was justly acclaimed for his portrayal of a Teddy-boy type – many feel that he stole the film.

'My Love'/'The Mess'
Apple R 5985. Produced: Paul and Linda McCartney
Released: March 24, 1973

By common consent, Paul McCartney has always excelled on straight rock 'n' roll songs – and, curiously, their antitheses: dreamy weepies. 'My Love' falls into the latter category, while the B-side is a fine example of the former.

With the Beatles' past royalties frozen by litigation, few money-making options remained to the former members of the group. The chief of these lay in writing songs that would be covered by other artists. 'My Love' is a classic example of such a song, positively oozing Manciniesque strings and the kind of sugary sentimentality that one finds either cloying or soothing.

'The Mess', in direct contrast, is a powerful stomper recorded live on a Wings tour. It features an intriguing echo-delay, clean production and slightly lacklustre drumming from Denny Seiwell.

THE BEATLES/1962–1966
Apple PCSP 717. Produced: George Martin
Released: May 5, 1973
Love Me Do (Paul)/Please Please Me (John)/From Me To You (John and Paul)/She Loves You (John and Paul)/I Want To Hold Your Hand (John and Paul)/All My Loving (Paul)/ Can't Buy Me Love (Paul)/A Hard Day's Night (John and Paul)/And I Love Her (Paul)/ Eight Days a Week (Paul)/I Feel Fine (John)/Ticket To Ride (John)/Yesterday (Paul)/Help! (John)/You've Got To Hide Your Love Away (John)/We Can Work It Out (Paul)/ Day Tripper (John and Paul)/Drive My Car (Paul)/Norwegian Wood (John)/Nowhere Man (John)/Michelle (Paul)/In My Life (John)/Girl (John)/Paperback Writer (Paul)/Eleanor Rigby (Paul)/ Yellow Submarine (Ringo)

THE BEATLES/1967–1970
Apple PCSP 718. Produced: George Martin and Phil Spector
Released: May 5, 1973
Strawberry Fields Forever (John)/Penny Lane (Paul)/Sgt Pepper's Lonely Hearts Club Band (John and Paul)/With a Little Help From My Friends (Ringo)/Lucy In the Sky With Diamonds (John)/A Day In the Life (John and Paul)/All You Need Is Love (John)/I Am the Walrus (John)/

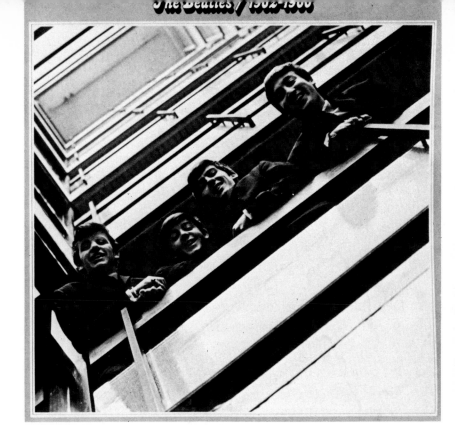

Hello Goodbye (Paul)/The Fool On the Hill (Paul)/Magical Mystery Tour (John and Paul)/ Lady Madonna (Paul)/Hey Jude (Paul)/Revolution (John)/Back In the USSR (Paul)/While My Guitar Gently Weeps (George)/Ob-La-Di, Ob-La-Da (Paul)/Get Back (Paul)/Don't Let Me Down (John)/The Ballad Of John & Yoko (John)/Old Brown Shoe (George)/Here Comes the Sun (George)/Come Together (John)/Something (George)/Octopus's Garden (Ringo)/Let It Be (Paul)/Across the Universe (John)/The Long and Winding Road (Paul)

Slowly accepting the fact that the Beatles existed no longer as a group, EMI issued this four-album cross-section of the better-known Beatle compositions, dating back to 'Love Me Do'. They were only just in time: an American 'pirate' compilation had been doing very brisk business for some weeks – it was advertised on the legitimate media – and fear of losing these lucrative sales may well have prompted the injured parties to issue their own version.

RED ROSE SPEEDWAY
Apple PCTC 251. Produced Paul McCartney
Released: May 5, 1973
Big Barn Bed/My Love/Get On the Right Thing/One More Kiss/Little Lamb Dragonfly/ Single Pigeon/When the Night/Loup (1st Indian On the Moon)/Medley: Hold Me Tight; Lazy Dynamite; Hands Of Love; Power Cut

This album occupies a curious place in the series of solo LPs made by McCartney since his first 'McCartney'. While unsatisfactory on many levels, it nonetheless represents a considerable improvement over 'Wild Life' and, with hindsight, can be seen as a crucial event in the McCartney's recording career. Itself undistinguished, it paved a reliable highway for the next, far superior, album.

McCartney's production is, again, far more painstaking than the quality of the material justifies – he had always been more imaginative than, say, Lennon, who'd found a satisfactory sound as far back as 'Plastic Ono Band' and stuck with it. This care can be heard on 'Big Barn Bed' and 'Little Lamb Dragonfly', plus the breezy 'One More Kiss'. A further interesting fact emerged: McCartney's often-forgotten ability as a bassist was strongly emphasised, to great effect, on all tracks.

The cynical might also observe that McCartney's credibility was further assisted by his arrest (for possession of drugs) shortly after the time of issue.

Top *A four-album compilation of the Beatles-that-are-no-more for the nostalgia market. The sleeve photos illustrate as well as the songs themselves the changes that eight years have wrought.*

Above *Sleeve for 'Red Rose Speedway'.*

105

Above *The peace gesture from George.*

Below right *Ringo in 1973.*

February
Rumours circulate that the Lennon's marriage is in trouble. *'We're facing a lot of emotional problems'*, says Yoko.

'People were offended when I married John. I think it would have been very different had I been an English girl.' Yoko Ono.

March 9
Paul fined £100 at Campbelltown for growing five cannabis plants in his Argyllshire greenhouse. Says Paul: *'I don't think it's dangerous. It should be like homosexuality — legal among consenting adults. But the Magistrate was sweet.'*

March 18
Wings play Release benefit at London's Hard-Rock Café.

'Give Me Love (Give Me Peace On Earth)'/'Miss O'Dell'
Apple R 5988. Produced: George Harrison
Released: May 26, 1973

Bearing more than a distant resemblance to Bob Dylan's 'I Want You', this is a somewhat plaintive ditty strongly featuring George's insubstantial voice and his excellent and highly idiosyncratic slide-guitar playing. But Harrison's very considerable following purchased it in droves, and duly caused it to reach a high position in the national charts. In fact, it was about the best song on the album.

'Live and Let Die'*/'I Lie Around'**
Apple R 5987. Produced: *George Martin; **Paul McCartney
Released: June 1, 1973

The James Bond movie of the same name provided Paul McCartney with a chance to exercise his flair for unusual work. His versatility and basic desire to be an all-round composer was to lead to less successful experiments than this effective and well-constructed piece of thriller theming. The mighty orchestral puncturings and the ghostly voices of Linda plus Wings guitarist Denny Laine merged with Paul's smooth vocal to create a genuine atmosphere of tension appropriate for 'A Licence To Kill'. The reggae'd section in the middle proved, once again, that McCartney had long ago mastered this idiom (remember 'Ob-la-di, Ob-la-da').

Bleating sheep and pastoral catcalls lead – somewhat whimsically – into the playful 'I Lie Around'. Nice harmonies. Forgettable tune. Having courageously laundered his smalls in public for the previous three years to great disadvantage, McCartney was now fast recovering his former self-confidence, and greater glories were shortly to follow.

LIVING IN THE MATERIAL WORLD
Apple PAS 10006. Produced: George Harrison
Released: June 9, 1973
Give Me Love (Give Me Peace On Earth)/Sue Me, Sue You Blues/The Light That Has Lighted the World/Don't Let Me Wait Too Long/Who Can See It/Living In the Material World/The Lord Loves the One (That Loves the Lord)/Try Some Buy Some/The Day the World Gets Round/That Is All

It is not the function of this book to comment on George Harrison's religious beliefs – so long as Harrison himself can refrain from didactically imposing said Holy Memoirs upon innocent record-collectors. Unfortunately, this is exactly what he did (to excess) on this LP, and therefore it seems fair to point out that Harrison's highly publicised beliefs seem to have brought him little joy. Indeed, it's difficult to see why he travelled all the way to India to import a God who, by the sound of him ('The Lord Loves the One Who Loves the Lord') is as intractable and selfish as the petulant Jehovah of Victorian Sunday schools.

Very little on this album commends itself. George's superb and accomplished slide-guitar breaks abound, but his thin vocals and the generally gloomy atmosphere dampen any spirits thus roused. The theme of the album is almost as offensive in its own way as Lennon's 'Some Time In New York City' – though Lennon at least contrived to lighten the heaviness of his lyrics by employing his peerless vocals; Harrison has no comparable talent, and 'Living In the Material World' can accordingly be dismissed.

'Photograph'*/'Down and Out'**
Apple R 5992. Produced: *Richard Perry; **George Harrison and Richard Perry
Released: October 20, 1973

In the hands of a skilful producer (like the ubiquitous Richard Perry) Ringo's talent has always repaid effort. Co-written with George Harrison, 'Photograph' displays strong affinities with the guitarist's distinctive composing style. It was released as a choice plum from the excellent 'Ringo' album that was to follow. Its flip side, 'Down and Out', is a very mundane throwaway tune only saved from extinction by the professional arrangement and by Harrison's distinctive slide-guitar solo.

'Helen Wheels'/'Country Dreamer'
Apple R 5993. Produced: Paul McCartney
Released: October 20, 1973

The quality on both sides of this charming little single reveals the McCartneys back from the wilderness and more than ready to take on all comers (including Ringo's 'Photograph', released the same day) in the chart arena. Ringo won – but this is probably due more to the dearth of good material from Paul in the previous two years than to the demerits of 'Helen Wheels'.

'Helen Wheels' is the nickname of the McCartneys' Land Rover; it bounces along in fairly impressive style – but the real charmer of this 45 is the cute 'Country Dreamer' which, although it takes four bars too long to get to the point, is a model of simplicity and a tasteful exercise in three-part harmony and clean unobtrusive production.

'Mind Games'/'Meat City'
Apple R 5994. Produced: John Lennon
Released: November 10, 1973

March
John Lennon ordered to leave US by Immigration Authorities. Replies Lennon: *'Having just celebrated our fourth wedding anniversary, we are not prepared to sleep in separate beds. Peace and Love, John and Yoko.'*

March
Ringo emphatic: chances of Beatle reunion absolutely out of the question.

March
Yoko wins custody of eight-year-old daughter Kyoko from ex-husband. But father Anthony Cox flees with child.

April
Paul intimates that he's not averse to a Beatle reunion.

Sleeve for 'Living in the Material World'.

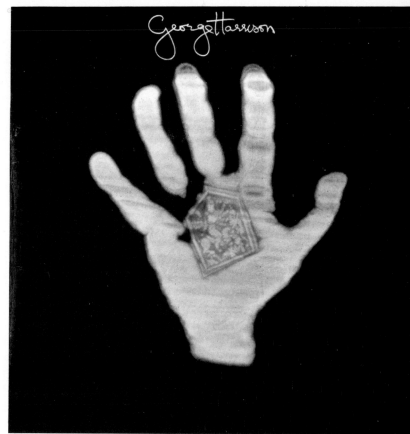

Above right Paul's TV *show, June 1973.*

April
ABKCO (Allen Klein) decline to renew contracts with John, George and Ringo.

June
Allen Klein sues John Lennon for $200,000 but John too busy fighting US deportation order to notice.

June 7
Transmission of 'James Paul McCartney' TV Special. Mixed reviews.

August 25
Henry McCullough quits Wings. Five days later, as group prepares to leave for extensive recording sessions in Lagos, Nigeria, drummer Denny Seiwell also hands in notice.

After the utter debâcle of 'Some Time In New York City', it was of crucial importance for John Lennon that his next issue be seen and recognised as a return to the melodicism of 'Imagine' and a rejection of the mindless militancy of the double album.

'Mind Games' partially succeeds. Musically, it could indeed be an 'Imagine' out-take; but lyrically, while avoiding the offensiveness of his previous album, it retreated too far into gormless wordage and thus failed to satisfy Lennon punters anxious for this gifted man to cease reacting to events and settle down to some serious song writing.

The B-side is a noise, rescued only by peerless unison guitars and a jived-up off-beat. Both tracks are from the 'Mind Games' LP.

MIND GAMES
Apple PCS 7165. Produced: John Lennon
Released: November 10, 1973
Mind Games/Tight Ass/Aisumasen (I'm Sorry)/One Day (At a Time)/Bring On the Lucie (Freeda People)/Nutopian International Anthem/Intuition/Out the Blue/Only People/I Know (I Know)/You Are Here/Meat City

This album bears all the hallmarks of being made without any definite objective in mind – other than to redeem the unpleasantness of 'Some Time In New York City'.

The title track has already been discussed (see above); 'Tight Ass', next to appear, is one of the best on the album, reeking of John's old cockiness and irreverence (perhaps his best qualities). These sentiments appear sporadically throughout the album (notably on 'Freeda People').

'You Are Here' is the only other track with anything special to commend it – in this case a pleasing use of near-muzak qualities (traditionally a Paul McCartney domain).

The production is nothing very special – particularly noticeable is the ending of Lennon's long partnership with Phil Spector – and the re-appearance of Lennon's heavily-reverbed vocal sound is less than imaginative. Musically, however, most of the cuts on 'Mind Games' are rich with unexplored chords and solos that never quite happen (or are lost in the mix). The main noteworthy point is a strong sense of melody: even if none of the tunes linger the way strong pop music should, the desire to return to the lyricism and melodic inventiveness of 'Imagine' is strongly apparent. The reasons the total album is not more effective can be laid at the door of Lennon's personal situation, and on his tendency to *react* to events, instead of *initiating* them.

RINGO
Apple PCTC 252. Produced: Richard Perry
Released: December 1973
I'm the Greatest/Have You Seen My Baby/Photograph/Sunshine Life For Me (Sail Away Raymond)/You're Sixteen/Oh My My/Step Lightly/Six O'Clock/Devil Woman/You and Me (Babe)

Ladies and Gentlemen, presenting Richard Starkey, MBE, doing what Richard Starkey, MBE, does best: crooning pure commercial pop kitsch, exquisitely produced by Richard Perry and ably assisted by innumerable talented friends, including Paul McCartney, MBE, George Harrison, MBE, John Lennon, MBE (retd.), Billy Preston, Klaus Voormann, Marc Bolan, Harry Nilsson, Jim Keltner, Bobby Keyes, Nicky Hopkins, Martha Reeves, Merry Clayton, Linda McCartney, Steve Cropper, David Bromberg and The Band.

It's still Ringo Starr's record.

'I'm the Greatest' (written by Lennon) is the nearest that the Beatles have recently come to finding themselves together in the same studio. The only one missing is Paul. It's interesting to note that the line-up on this track – Lennon, Harrison, Ringo, Voormann and Preston – was allegedly considered as the New Beatles personnel (with the addition of Nilsson) when McCartney handed in his notice. Not surprisingly, it is the most Beatlesque cut on the album, with economical bass figures, jangling guitar arpeggios (and a wicked little flashback to 'Sgt Pepper' therein). Harrison's hoe-down 'Sunshine Life For Me' is fairly weak melodically, and its only interesting facet is the presence of master-musicians The Band on various country instruments.

'Oh My My' is a straight disco thumper with fatback brass and chirping girlie choir. Sandwiched in between the obvious commercial tracks are songs like 'Step Lightly' which would have slotted in perfectly on the 'White Album', and there is some nice use of laconic horns, Steve Cropper's delicate guitar and Ringo's nimble feet.

The McCartneys' contribution to this bill of fare ('Six O'Clock') is laced with some very competent synthesiser, block harmonies and a melody that grows in best pop style. 'Devil Woman' is out of the same brash mould as 'Oh My My', while the finale 'You and Me (Babe)' is used largely as a framework for a heartfelt thank-you speech from the Starr of the show to all those concerned – and it works without being schmaltzy.

November John, Paul and George sue Allen Klein. December After innumerable refusals, McCartney is granted a US Visa.	*'The only thing that has prevented us from getting together again has been Klein's contractual hold over the Beatles' name; when he is out of the way, there is no real reason why we shouldn't get together again.'* Paul McCartney.

Top *John in 1973, no longer in political 'uniform'.*

Above *Sleeve for 'Ringo'.*

1974

January
Yet more speculation in the press of a Beatles reunion. In Los Angeles Lennon says: *'I think anything is possible now and if it happens, I'm sure we'll all do something wonderful'.* While at the same time the New York-based McCartney adds: *'We wouldn't get together as the Beatles, but I'd like to see us working together — possibly for recording — and I think we will.'* Harrison and Starr remain silent.

January
Lennon asks the Queen for a Royal Pardon in connection with his five-year-old drug conviction, so as to be free to travel to and from the United States. Says Lennon: *'It has left me with a criminal record.'*

February
Harrison in India buying many Things Holy. Including statue of Goddess Kali.

BAND ON THE RUN
Apple PAS 10007. Produced: Paul McCartney
Released: January 1974
Band On the Run/Jet/Bluebird/Mrs Vandebilt/Let Me Roll It/Mamunia/No Words/Picasso's Last Words (Drink To Me)/Nineteen Hundred and Eighty-five

If Paul McCartney had been, as we have stated, in the wilderness for the previous three years, this magnificent album certainly re-instated him in the public eye and in the eyes of the numerous critics who had long previously dismissed his talent as 'lightweight' and 'over-stylised'. *Rolling Stone* wrote: 'McCartney . . . walking a middle ground between autobiographical song writing and subtle attempts to mythologise his own experience through the creation of a fantasy world of adventure – perhaps remotely inspired by his having recently written "Live And Let Die". He does it by uniting the myth of the rock star and the outlaw, the original legendary figure On The Run.'

Well . . . perhaps so. For the authors of this book, McCartney's main achievement here was to record an album under what can only be described as calamitous conditions: Wings guitarist Henry McCullough and drummer Denny Seiwell departed while 'Band On the Run' was still in the planning stage; undaunted, the McCartneys, plus faithful Denny Laine, continued with the recording (Laine playing lead guitar, McCartney playing drums) and came up with what is incomparably Wings' best album to date – and the best album (apart from, possibly, Lennon's 'Plastic Ono Band') recorded by any ex-Beatle. The result was that his critics were overnight forced to revise their opinions as to his future.

So what is this album? It reveals McCartney, not unnaturally, producing what McCartney produces best: disciplined arrangements; a strong sense of melody allied to a natural feel for exotic rhythms, the whole thing coupled to a resurgence of self-confidence. He also avoids the use of Beatle stylistic devices: devices are certainly present, but they are McCartney's personal property, and on 'Band On the Run' he uses them in a perfectly satisfactory manner.

Humour is also present: in (long-delayed) answer to Lennon's cruel 'How Do You Sleep' ('Imagine' LP), Paul fights back – gently – with a beautiful and totally sympathetic impersonation of Lennon's own idiosyncratic vocal/production style, 'Let Me Roll It' (complete with Arthur Janov-style primal whimper at the close). The understatement of this track contrasts with Lennon's misplaced viciousness to a marked degree.

Though 'Let Me Roll It' is the track which attracted most attention, many others stand out. 'Jet', which shortly afterwards became a single, is a thundering piece, featuring obscure lyrics and McCartney's own matchless bass; he also plays Moog synthesiser with more taste than most other exponents of this Frankensteinian instrument. His lightweight touch (which has only proved successful when allied to his natural ebullience) works superbly on 'Bluebird' (which recalls 'Blackbird' from 'The White Album') and on 'Mrs Vandebilt' – where Paul asks *'What's the use of worrying?'*. *'No use'* he answers himself, and, of course, he's dead right. In fact, it's the self-confidence of this album – especially after his many years in disfavour – which is so refreshing.

It was perhaps this very self-confidence which enabled him to tackle 'Picasso's Last Words' (allegedly *'Drink to me – drink to my health'*). Actor Dustin Hoffman was on hand when Paul first began writing this song, and the preliminary tracks (like much of 'Band On the Run') were recorded at drummer Ginger Baker's ARC studio in Lagos, Nigeria. The title track, 'Band On the Run' itself, is the source of much speculation as to Hidden Meaning – but the real truth is likely to be that McCartney, as always, was experimenting with words that had a pleasing sound and convenient scansion; the track is briefly reprised at the end of the album in best 'Sgt Pepper' style.

Left Sleeve for Paul's 'Band on the Run'.

'You're Sixteen'/'Devil Woman'
Apple R 5995. Produced: Richard Perry
Released: February 11, 1974

A further brace of tracks lifted from the million-plus selling 'Ringo' album gave Mr Starkey his second smash single from his all-Beatle LP. Quite like old times.

Ringo warbles the old Johnny Burnette hit in a completely personal way, assisted by Harry Nilsson (shoo-wops) and Paul McCartney (kazoo). It may not be a guide to 1974 pop music but, like almost everything that Ringo has turned his hand to, it's a real indication of where the drummin' man's affinities have always lain.

'Jet'/'Let Me Roll It'
Apple R 5996. Produced: Paul McCartney
Released: February 18, 1974

There is such an abundance of truly fine music to be found on both sides of 'Band On the Run' that it must have been difficult for McCartney to decide upon a single.

Temporarily avoiding the title track (which as it transpires was to prove his biggest-ever selling single when public demand dictated), Paul astutely plumbed for 'Jet', with its hard-hitting brashness and easy-to-assimilate hook-line.

'Band On the Run'/'Zoo Gang'
Apple R 5997. Produced: Paul McCartney
Released: June 28, 1974

The title track of Paul McCartney's supreme solo achievement from an album which achieved the unique distinction of recapturing the Number One slot on the US album chart on no less than three separate occasions. Not even the Beatles managed that feat!

'Zoo Gang' again reveals McCartney's lucrative sideline of knocking off neat little themes for the screen. This time the television screen.

February
Press reports insist that John and Yoko have split. The fact that Yoko is in New York pursuing a solo career while John is in Los Angeles escorting May Pang (referred to as 'The 1974 Yoko') only help to fan the flames.

March
After throwing insults at the Smothers Brothers and punches at their manager and a cocktail waitress, John Lennon is physically removed from Los Angeles' famed Troubadour Club. Following fracas, Naomi the injured waitress states: *'It's not the pain that hurts; it's finding out that one of your idols is a real asshole.'*

June
George Harrison announces the formation of his own Dark Horse record label to be distributed worldwide by A & M Records. First signing, you guessed it, Ravi Shankar.

Left *George announces the formation of his new label and the US concert tour.* Above *Promotion sticker for 'Jet'.*

Sleeve for 'Walls and Bridges'.

112

'Whatever Gets You Thru the Night'/'Beef Jerky'
Apple R 5998 Produced: John Lennon
Released: October 5, 1974

Perhaps this single's most interesting quality is its almost total anonymity. It is catchy, well-played, jerky, poppy – and it could have been recorded by almost anyone, including John Lennon. The approach, in fact, might have been culled direct from Paul McCartney, but the studio feel, and more especially the honking tenor of Bobby Keys, are definitely American. And the Lennon lavatory voice is beginning to vanish. This single also marks the first recorded appearance of Lennon's partnership (in the loosest sense) with Elton John.

WALLS AND BRIDGES
Apple PCTC 253 Produced: John Lennon
Released: October 5, 1974

Going Down On Love/Whatever Gets You Thru the Night/Old Dirt Road/What You Got/
Bless You/Scared/No. 9 Dream/Surprise, Surprise (Sweet Bird Of Paradox)/Steel and Glass/
Beef Jerky/Nobody Loves You (When You're Down and Out)/Ya Ya

By his own admission 'Mind Games' (the previous LP) was a transitionary period for Lennon. And it must be said that JL has never, ever been shy of exposing his Transitionary Periods to an increasingly sceptical public. 'Walls and Bridges', his most recent album to date, betrays – if anything – that Lennon's Transitionary Period is now somewhat overstretched. The album is generally lacklustre, though it has sold well and has been greeted by more sympathetic reviews than any Lennon product since 'Imagine'. And, like 'Mind Games', the album tends to grow on one and relieve, to some extent, the initial sense of disappointment.

Few of the tracks reveal anything about the new Lennon: the lyrics – though vaguely identifiable with sentiments expressed by their composer in the past – seem mechanical, cranked-out, like well-worn conversational gambits. But the voice is in abrasive form, and of course the musicianship is excellent. Perhaps (as was hoped after 'Mind Games') this LP represents a further water-treading period for Lennon, and shortly he'll re-emerge in full flower to re-establish himself among the upper echelons once more. Opinions differ.

'Junior's Farm'/'Sally G'
Apple R5999 Produced: Paul McCartney
Released: October 26, 1974

McCartney's first record for nearly a year – and by the time it emerged 'Band on the Run' had sold nearly six million copies worldwide. Out to prove he can write rockers, McCartney rolls out a fat-sounding four-in-the-bar thumper which recalls, more than anything, his earlier 'Get Back'. And on these merits, the re-vibed Wings line-up must finally be accepted as a valid band in its own right – and not merely as a vehicle for an ex-Beatle. Yes, he can write rockers.

'Only You'/'Call Me'
Apple R 6000. Produced: Richard Perry
Released: November 16, 1974

Ringo (plus Lennon, plus Billy Preston) digs deep into his personal chestnut sack to produce a reggaefied remake of the old Platters' hit. Memphis guitarist Steve Cropper guests. The production is cluttered, but the odd contrast between the vocal demands made by the song and Ringo's patent inability to match them is somehow endearing.

GOODNIGHT VIENNA
Apple PCS 7168. Produced: Richard Perry
Released: November 16, 1974

**(It's All Da-Da-Down To) Goodnight Vienna/Occapella/Oo-Wee/Husbands and Wives/
Snookeroo/All By Myself/Call Me/No No Song/Only You/Easy For Me/Goodnight Vienna
(Reprise)**

Ringo's first album since his much-praised 'Ringo' set. To reproduce the success, the same
ingredients (more or less) were chosen – i.e., zads of guest-stars including as many ex-Beatles
as possible (to give the LP 'the aura of . . . an ersatz Beatle album', as a critic remarked at
time of issue). Yet the overall impression is of a lesser opus. It fails mainly because Ringo is
no judge of his own best material, and because producer Richard Perry has underestimated
The Nose by piling on layers of surfeit sound (choirs etc.), until the album loses personality.

The greater misjudgments occur when Ringo over-emotionalises numbers (such as Harry
Nilsson's 'Easy For Me') without adding the also-necessary ingredient of hamminess.
Humour does cut through saccharine, and Ringo's natural forte *is* humour, after all. Some
songs are simply dull ('Call Me') and others are gormless ('Husbands and Wives'), and only
four really cut through the deep-pile carpet-clippings: 'Goodnight Vienna' (written by
Lennon), 'Occapella' (Allen Toussaint), 'Snookeroo' (Elton John and Bennie Taupin) and
Hoyt Axton's hilarious 'No No Song' – the best of its genre since 'Cigareets 'n whisky 'n
wild, wild wimmin'.

Well, four good songs on an album means you make it on the percentages but lose out on
the bonuses. From a man who's not really expected to prove anything, that's still good value.

'Ding Dong'/'I Don't Care Anymore'
Apple R 6002. Produced: George Harrison
Released: December 13, 1974

The George Harrison Christmas Single (in Britain only). There were harsh words said of
this particular waxing at time of issue, and we can sadly find little fault with the opinions
expressed. 'Ding Dong' is meticulously-played emptiness, a charmless reworking of the
traditional peal o' bells (with a choir singing, you guessed, 'Ding dong ding dong' etc); while
trite lyrics ('Ring out the old, ring in the new') occasionally surface. A pox on it.

DARK HORSE
Apple PAS 10008. Produced: George Harrison
Released: December 13, 1974
**Hari's On Tour (Express)/Simply Shady/So Sad/Bye Bye, Love/Maya Love/Ding Dong, Ding
Dong/Dark Horse/Far East Man/It Is 'He' (Jai Sri Krishna)**

This LP is presented to the purchaser with a self-pitying slab of sub-Desiderata penned
around the inner-sleeve margins: an appeal to critics to treat the album with care, for it was
made 'most for thy pleasure'.

So it may have been – but if so then it signally fails in its purpose. Perhaps worse even than
'Material World', 'Dark Horse' reveals that Harrison possesses that peculiar quality of
stubbornness which interprets (as a reflex) all criticisms of his work as Godless Mouthings,
mainly to be pitied. And so he gives the listener his pity, and his condescension – as he did
on the previous album – and the overall effect is quite incredibly annoying.

It is, of course, only a coincidence that 'Dark Horse' is also the title of George Harrison's
recently-launched record label.

What can be said for the album? For those who believe in ostentatious holiness, it no doubt
has a congratulatory quality. And musically, the playing is impeccable (but so it is on most
albums in these latter days). But the lyrics are, in turn, sanctimonious, repetitive, vituperative
and self-satisfied. It is a boring album. One wishes that it had not come from an ex-Beatle.

Top *Ringo's latest album to date.*

Above *And George's.* 113

July 26–28
Joe Pope's Strawberry Fields Forever Fan Club organises the first Beatle Convention in Boston. An equally well-attended second Beatlefest is staged in New York a couple of months later.

August 15
Beatle musical *John, Paul, George, Ringo . . . and Bert* opens at London's Lyric Theatre to rave reviews.

September
The Board of Immigration Appeals orders Lennon to leave the US voluntarily by September 8, 1974, or be deported. Lennon chooses third alternative and lodges yet another appeal.

October
George Harrison confirms that his marriage to Patti Boyd is on the rocks and that Patti is now 'just good friends' with Eric Clapton.

November
Ringo Starr confirms that his marriage to Maureen is in difficulty. Press hint at a divorce.

November
Beatle musical *Sgt Pepper's Lonely Hearts Club Band on the Road* opens to excellent reviews at New York's Beacon Theatre.

December
John Lennon joins Elton John on stage at Madison Square Garden to jam on 'Whatever Gets You Thru The Night', 'Lucy In The Sky With Diamonds' and 'I Saw Her Standing There'.

Top right *The new Wings line-up. Flanking Paul and Linda are, left to right: Geoff Britten, Jimmy McCulloch and Denny Laine.*

Right *John jamming with Elton John at Madison Square Garden.*

Above *The new Beatle musical opens in New York.*

THE OUTRO

Above *Paul and Linda, 1973,*

and *George in 1974.*

There are few reasons why the Beatles should not be able to re-form – if they wish to. The possibility that they might actually do so is still very much a going concern in music business circles, and it's frequently pointed out that the only theoretical obstacle to such a reunion are legal formalities which could, if desired, be swept away at a moment's notice.

Whether this much looked-for event is actually *likely* to occur is another matter altogether. There seem to be three possibilities: that the Beatles will re-form *as the Beatles*; that a *de facto* Beatles might appear under some other name; and, most likely, that no reunion – on a permanent basis – will take place at all.

Shortly before his death in 1967, Brian Epstein told an interviewer: 'They will not always be together and they are already cutting their own fork roads. But I cannot see them ever breaking links with one another. Their interests are too kindred. They will always inspire each other.'

This is not quite as apt as it was in 1967, but even then the group had already shared so many experiences common to them alone that it seems hard to believe they will sever the links that bound them for so long.

But maintaining contact is a long step from actual re-formation. 'As far as getting together as we were, as the Beatles were', said Paul McCartney in January 1974, 'I don't think that'll ever happen again . . . but there might be things . . . ventures . . . mutually helpful to all of us . . . things people would like to see.'

It was Paul, of course, who initiated the 'official' disintegration of the group by suing the other three Beatles 'as the only way to sue Allen Klein' (January 1973). His foresight and business judgment have since been vindicated to some extent, but at the same time he came in for much hostility from fellow-Beatles and public alike. 'Paul acted like a spoilt child', said Ringo during the court hearings, but Paul also showed a *prima facie* case and, as he'd wished, the Beatles' assets (including considerable 'frozen' royalties from past record sales) were put in the hands of the Official Receiver.

Immediately following the successful conclusion of his civil action, McCartney entered a bleak period of isolation (from all except wife Linda) and low-standard creativity. His first solo album, 'McCartney', failed to impress to any great extent, and his second, 'Ram', recorded during and after the hearings, was defensively low-level in aim. Critics recalled the old objections to McCartney's music – his obsession with style and his distressing predilection for *schmaltz* – and noted that his music now possessed more of these qualities than formerly.

Doggedly, McCartney stuck to his declared aim of forming an altogether new group (as if he felt compelled to demonstrate that the Beatles were indeed finished). He succeeded in doing so and launched his new band Wings with a poor album, 'Wild Life', and a curious incognito university tour. Though the group contained several excellent musicians (McCartney himself is a first-class and highly under-rated bassist), they failed to attract serious critical attention – until recently, when Paul McCartney emerged from his long day's night with an excellent album, 'Band On the Run'.

Paul has always been the most outspoken against re-forming the group. As the initiator of its (official) dissolution he presumably still has a point to support but there can be little doubt that he would oppose any *official* re-formed Beatles. Yet he would certainly have to be included: the Lennon-McCartney axis was the core of the Beatles' success, and it would be unthinkable to conceive of a re-formed group without McCartney.

If Paul took longest to recover from an event he himself had initiated, then others were quicker off the mark. George Harrison was the first Beatle to produce a solo album of any sort ('Wonderwall Music', November 1968), but it was his third, 'All Things Must Pass', made with care and immaculate timing after the break-up, which acquired for him the kind of prestige he'd always wanted. George used this sudden flowering of acclaim in a particularly creative way, by organising – at great personal effort – the triumphant Bangla Desh concerts in New York's Madison Square Garden (July, 1971).

George Harrison's character is often misunderstood, but his religious convictions are well known – as is his devotion to the culture of the Indian sub-continent. His piety is frequently the target of acid comment, but there can be little doubt of the sincerity. Though Harrison's beliefs seem nowadays to stifle rather than stimulate him, he stays on the fringes, playing the occasional international session under one of his many pseudonyms, and donating the money so earned to various charities. Despite some failures and a rather weak album, 'Living In the Material World', George's status is still high, and he has always been a creative and original guitarist.

His attitude to a possible re-formation of the Beatles is now known to be unfavourable – in any case in view of the huge success which came his way with 'All Things Must Pass' and the Bangla Desh concerts, it is highly debatable whether he could ever be content with the semi-subservient role he occupied in the original group.

If Harrison's progress has drooped somewhat in recent months then Ringo Starr's has been a steady and unadventurous climb from the affection accorded the Lovable Nose to genuine respect as a light entertainer. Always a comfortable person, Ringo, when left to himself, opted almost immediately for the equally comfortable country and western beloved of Liverpool Irish clubs and easy-going people everywhere.

Ringo's post-Beatle years have been spent in movie acting and directing and, like George, in exclusive session work. Unlike George, he keeps his money. In 1969 Starr emphatically vetoed prospects for re-formation. As far as is known, his current opinions are unchanged.

Few will disagree that John Lennon is probably the most gifted of the four original Beatles. More flukey, too, more emotional – and certainly more dependent on the approval of others.

His progress since the dissolution has also been the most erratic and certainly the most interesting. Prolific with solo albums since the beginning of his relationship with Yoko Ono, Lennon has made at least two (and possibly three) 'solo' LPs which stand among the Beatles' greatest recorded achievements.

The final year of the Beatles' existence and the first year of their non-'existence' saw Lennon in fine form: 'Live Peace In Toronto', 'Plastic Ono Band' and 'Imagine' are all good albums, and the final two can be seen as a series on one theme. John seemed to have evolved – after three years of endearing grotesque antics – a steady line of progression and a firmly defined musical identity.

Following 'Imagine', Lennon's ideals took a sharp swerve from the pacifist *avant-garde* to the committed militance of 1971–72 New York radical-chic society. His sincere peace crusading (as real and necessary to Lennon as evangelism is to Billy Graham) was replaced by the angry rhetoric and sloganised cantos which infect 'artistic' ghettos everywhere. He encapsulated his new-found fire in a disastrous LP, 'Sometime In New York City', which, though it didn't detract too much from his immense accumulated respect, lowered his own musical and lyrical standards to abysmal levels. Though perhaps predictable, this shattering downfall of Lennon's unhappily seems to have ushered in a period of little creativity and apparent discontinuity. A brawl in the Los Angeles Troubadour Club showed him in a poor light; his domestic situation is reportedly in troubled waters; he cannot leave the United States because he may then never be able to return, owing to his British drug convictions. Yet he remains the most talented of the four.

John Lennon has always been particularly ambiguous on the subject of a possible Beatle reunion. Certainly his bitter vendetta against Paul McCartney precluded it until fairly recently – but Lennon himself has now filed a lawsuit against Allen Klein, the target of Paul McCartney's initial action, so the differences separating the two most indispensable Beatles may not be very great after all. Lennon's remarks on the subject have always left provisos open, options available, ends to be picked up. (He could probably also use the cash, having been overwhelmingly and quite foolishly generous in the past three years.)

It is the financial incentives which offer the most likely inducements for a (*de facto* or otherwise) Beatles re-formation. The frozen assests are sure to be very considerable – a reformation of the group would, theoretically, release this cash. And a reorganised Beatles could quite certainly write its own cheque from any recording company in the world – they would still be worth far more collectively than individually.

Ringo in the early '70s, and John in 1974, still exiled in New York.

American Releases

'I Want To Hold Your Hand' (Capitol 5112), was the first Beatle single to bring the group into (US) national prominence. Prior to this, the Beatles material had been released on a variety of labels without any positive reaction. The Vee-Jay material was re-packaged innumerable times. First as 'Introducing The Beatles – England's No. 1 Vocal Group' (VJLP 1062) and thereafter in various permutations.

'Please Please Me', 'Ask Me Why', 'From Me To You' and 'Thank You Girl' reappeared on an album padded out by some 'live' Frank Ifield hits entitled 'Jolly, What!' (VJLP 1085). With 'Please Please Me' and 'Ask Me Why' replacing 'Love Me Do' and 'PS I Love You', the 'Introducing the Beatles' album was hastily coupled with a collection of Four Seasons hits and issued as a bizarre double album called 'The Beatles vs The Four Seasons' (VJDX 30). Finally, the 'Introducing' album was re-sleeved and re-titled 'The Beatles – Songs, Pictures & Stories' (VJLP 1092).

The Vee-Jay singles were later to be incorporated as part of the 'Oldies 45' re-issue series before Vee-Jay finally went out of business. Likewise, the material that the Beatles had recorded in Hamburg with Tony Sheridan for Polydor became scattered over a number of various labels. 'Ain't She Sweet', 'Sweet Georgia Brown', 'Nobody's Child' and 'Take Out Some Insurance On Me Baby' were collated as 'Ain't She Sweet And Other Great Group Sounds From England' (Atco 33–169). 'My Bonnie', 'Why', 'Cry For a Shadow' and 'The Saints' almost simultaneously appeared on 'My Bonnie' (MGM ESE 4215) and later as 'This Is Where It All Started' (Metro 563 – an MGM subsidiary). The Atco album resurfaced again under the guise of 'The Amazing Beatles' (Clarion 601), while other cuts were presented as 'The Savage Young Beatles' (Savage BM 69).

In other words, it was all extremely confusing for American Beatlemaniacs.

'INTRODUCING THE BEATLES – England's No. 1 Vocal Group'
Vee-Jay VJLP 1062
I Saw Her Standing There/Misery/Anna/ Chains/Boys/Love Me Do/ P.S. I Love You/Baby It's You/ Do You Want to Know a Secret?/A Taste of Honey/ There's a Place/Twist and Shout

'Please Please Me'/'Ask Me Why'
Vee-Jay 498

'From Me To You'/'Thank You Girl'
Vee-Jay 522

'Please Please Me'/'From Me To You'
Vee-Jay 581

'Do You Want To Know a Secret?'/ 'Thank You Girl'
Vee-Jay 587

Misery/Taste of Honey/Anna/Ask Me Why
Vee-Jay EP 1–903

'She Loves You'/'I'll Get You'
Swan 4152

'Sie Liebt Dich'/'I'll Get You'
Swan 4182

'Twist and Shout'/'There's a Place'
Tollie 9001

'Love Me Do'/'P.S. I Love You'
Tollie 9008

'Sweet Georgia Brown'/'Take Out Some Insurance On Me Baby'
Atco 6302

'Ain't She Sweet'/'Nobody's Child'
Atco 6308

'My Bonnie'/'The Saints'
MGM 13213

'Cry For a Shadow'/'Why?'
MGM 13227

CAPITOL 6000 SERIES
Following the overwhelming success of their first two Beatle releases 'I Want To Hold Your Hand' (Jan '64) and 'Can't Buy Me Love' (March '64), Capitol Records acquired all the earlier Beatle product that had been initially leased to the Vee-Jay, Tollie and Swan labels. So as not to miss out on escalating sales or mess up the continuity of new product and their catalogue numbers, Capitol hurriedly re-released these tracks (and more) via their 6000 Series throughout the earlier part of 1964.

'Twist and Shout'/'There's a Place'
Capitol 6061 (Originally Tollie 9001)

'PS I Love You'/'Love Me Do'
Capitol 6062 (Originally Tollie 9008)

'Please Please Me'/'From Me To You'
Capitol 6063 (Originally Vee-Jay 581)

'Do You Want To Know a Secret?'/'Thank You Girl'
Capitol 6064 (Originally Vee-Jay 587)

'Roll Over Beethoven'/'Misery'
Capitol 6065

'All My Loving'/'This Boy'
Capitol 6066

CHRONOLOGICAL RELEASES IN AMERICA: CAPITOL/APPLE

'I Want To Hold Your Hand'/'I Saw Her Standing There'
Capitol 5112
Released: January 13, 1964

MEET THE BEATLES
Capitol ST 2047
Released: January 20, 1964
I Want To Hold Your Hand/I Saw Her Standing There/This Boy/It Won't be Long/All I've Got To Do/All My Loving/Don't Bother Me/Little Child/Till There Was You/Hold Me Tight/I Wanna Be Your Man/Not a Second Time

'Can't Buy Me Love'/'You Can't Do That'
Capitol 5150
Released: March 30, 1964

THE BEATLES SECOND ALBUM
Capitol ST 2080
Released: April 10, 1964
Roll Over Beethoven/Thank You Girl/You Really Got a Hold On Me/Devil In Her Heart/Money/You Can't Do That/Long Tall Sally/I Call Your Name/Please Mr Postman/I'll Get You/She Loves You

Roll Over Beethoven/All My Loving/This Boy/Please Mr Postman
Capitol EAP–2121
Released: May 11, 1964

A HARD DAY'S NIGHT
United Artists UAS 3366A
Released: June 26, 1964
A Hard Day's Night/Tell Me Why/I'll Cry Instead/I Should Have Known Better (instrumental)/I'm Happy Just To Dance With You/And I Love Her (instrumental)/I Should Have Known Better/If I Fell/And I Love Her/Ringo's Theme – This Boy (instrumental)/Can't Buy Me Love/A Hard Day's Night (instrumental)

'A Hard Day's Night'/'I Should Have Known Better'
Capitol 5222
Released: July 13, 1964

'I'll Cry Instead'/'I'm Happy Just To Dance With You'
Capitol 5234
Released: July 20, 1964

'And I Love Her'/'If I Fell'
Capitol 5235
Released: July 20, 1964

'Something New'
Capitol ST 2108
Released: July 20, 1964
I'll Cry Instead/Things We Said Today/Any Time At All/When I Get Home/Slow Down/Matchbox/Tell Me Why/And I Love Her/I'm Happy Just To Dance With You/If I Fell/Komm, Gib Mir Deine Hand (I Want To Hold Your Hand)

'Slow Down'/'Matchbox'
Capitol 5255
Released: August 24, 1964

'I Feel Fine'/'She's a Woman'
Capitol 5327
Released: November 23, 1964

THE BEATLES STORY
Capitol STBO 2222
Released: November 23, 1964
On Stage With the Beatles/How Beatlemania Began/Beatlemania In Action/Man Behind the Beatles – Brian Epstein/John Lennon/Who's a Millionaire?/ Beatles Will Be Beatles/Man Behind the Music – George Martin/George Harrison/A Hard Day's Night/Their First Movie/Paul McCartney/Sneaky Haircuts and More About Paul/The Beatles Look At Life/'Victims' Of Beatlemania/Beatle Medley/Ringo Starr/Liverpool and All the World!

BEATLES '65
Capitol ST 2228
Released: December 15, 1964
No Reply/I'm a Loser/Baby's In Black/Rock and Roll Music/I'll Follow the Sun/Mr Moonlight/Honey Don't/I'll Be Back/ /She's a Woman/I Feel Fine/Everybody's Trying To Be My Baby

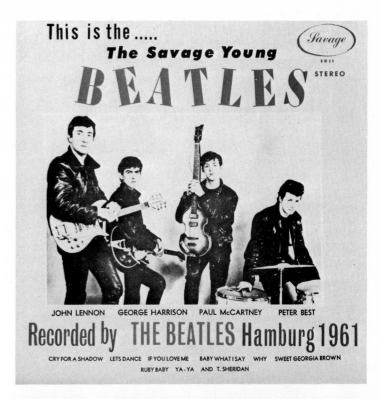

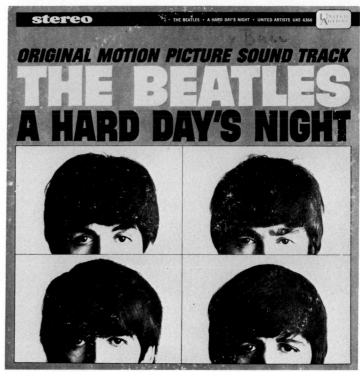

Honey Don't/I'm a Loser/Mr Moonlight/Everybody's Trying To Be My Baby
Capitol 5365
Released: February 1, 1965

119

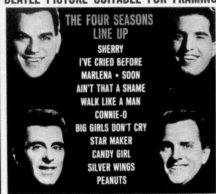

THE INTERNATIONAL BATTLE OF THE CENTURY

TWO RECORD SET

THE Beatles VS THE FOUR SEASONS

VEE-JAY RECORDS

EACH DELIVERING THEIR GREATEST VOCAL PUNCHES

INSIDE: SCORECARDS, BIOGRAPHIES, PICTURES, STORIES OF ALL THE CONTESTANTS
PLUS: FREE BONUS 8˝ X 15˝ FULL COLOR BEATLE PICTURE SUITABLE FOR FRAMING

BEATLES LINE UP
I SAW HER STANDING THERE
MISERY · ANNA
CHAINS · BOYS
ASK ME WHY
PLEASE, PLEASE ME
BABY IT'S YOU
DO YOU WANT TO KNOW A SECRET
A TASTE OF HONEY
THERE'S A PLACE
TWIST AND SHOUT

THE FOUR SEASONS LINE UP
SHERRY
I'VE CRIED BEFORE
MARLENA · SOON
AIN'T THAT A SHAME
WALK LIKE A MAN
CONNIE-O
BIG GIRLS DON'T CRY
STAR MAKER
CANDY GIRL
SILVER WINGS
PEANUTS

YOU BE THE JUDGE AND JURY!

DX 30

CAPITOL FULL DIMENSIONAL STEREO

THE BEATLES' STORY

A NARRATIVE AND MUSICAL BIOGRAPHY OF BEATLEMANIA ON 2 LONG-PLAY RECORDS

includes
SELECTIONS FROM THEIR HIT RECORDS
INTERVIEWS WITH THE BEATLES AND THEIR FANS
MANY NEW PHOTOS
THEIR WHOLE STORY ON RECORD... FROM BEGINNING TO FABULOUS FAME!

Capitol RECORDS HIGH FIDELITY

'Eight Days a Week'/'I Don't Want To Spoil the Party'
Capitol 5371
Released: February 15, 1965

THE EARLY BEATLES
Capitol ST 2309
Released: March 22, 1965
Love Me Do/ Twist and Shout/Anna/
Chains/Boys/Ask Me Why/Please, Please
Me/P.S. I Love You/Baby It's You/
A Taste Of Honey/Do You Want To
Know a Secret?

'Ticket To Ride'/'Yes It Is'
Capitol 5407
Released: April 19, 1965

BEATLES VI
Capitol ST 2358
Released: June 14, 1965
Kansas City/Eight Days a Week/You
Like Me Too Much/Bad Boy/I Don't
Want To Spoil the Party/Words Of Love/
What You're Doing/ Yes It is/Dizzy Miss
Lizzy/Tell Me What You See/Every Little
Thing

'Help!'/'I'm Down'
Capitol 5476
Released: July 19, 1965

HELP!
Capitol SMAS 2386
Released: August 13, 1965
Help!/The Night Before/From Me To You
Fantasy (instrumental)/You've Got To
Hide Your Love Away/I Need You/In
the Tyrol (instrumental)/Another Girl/
Another Hard Day's Night (instrumental)
/Ticket To Ride/The Bitter End – You
Can't Do That (instrumental)/You're
Going To Lose That Girl/The Chase
(instrumental)

'Act Naturally'/'Yesterday'
Capitol 5498
Released: September 13, 1965

See page 119.

See page 119.

'Day Tripper'/'We Can Work It Out'
Capitol 5555
Released: December 6, 1965

RUBBER SOUL
Capitol ST 2442
Released: December 6, 1965
I've Just Seen a Face/Norwegian Wood/
You Won't See Me/Think For Yourself/
The Word/Michelle/It's Only Love/Girl/
I'm Looking Through You/In My Life/
Wait/Run For Your Life.

'Nowhere Man'/'What Goes On'
Capitol 5587
Released: February 7, 1966

'Paperback Writer'/'Rain'
Capitol 5651
Released: May 23, 1966

YESTERDAY . . . AND TODAY
Capitol ST 2553
Released: June 15, 1966
Drive My Car/I'm Only Sleeping/
Nowhere Man/Dr Robert/Yesterday/Act
Naturally/And Your Bird Can Sing/If I
Needed Someone/We Can Work It Out/
What Goes On?/Day Tripper

'Yellow Submarine'/'Eleanor Rigby'
Capitol 5715
Released: August 8, 1966

REVOLVER
Capitol ST 2576
Released: August 8, 1966
Taxman/Eleanor Rigby/Love You To/
Here, There and Everywhere/Yellow
Submarine/She Said, She Said/Good Day
Sunshine/For No One/I Want To Tell You
/Got To Get You Into My Life/Tomorrow
Never Knows

'Strawberry Fields Forever'/'Penny Lane'
Capitol 5810
Released: February 13, 1967

**'SERGEANT PEPPER'S LONELY
HEARTS CLUB BAND'**
Capitol SMAS 2653
Released: June 2, 1967

**'All You Need Is Love'/'Baby, You're a
Rich Man'**
Capitol 5964
Released: July 24, 1967

'Hello Goodbye'/'I Am the Walrus'
Capitol 2056
Released: November 27, 1967

'MAGICAL MYSTERY TOUR'
Capitol SMAL 2835
Released: November 27, 1967
Magical Mystery Tour/The Fool On the
Hill/Flying/Blue Jay Way/Your Mother
Should Know/I Am the Walrus/Hello
Goodbye/Strawberry Fields Forever/
Penny Lane/Baby, You're a Rich Man/All
You Need Is Love

'Lady Madonna'/'The Inner Light'
Capitol 2138

Above *Artwork for the American 'Help!' sleeve.*

Released: March 18, 1968

'Hey Jude'/'Revolution'
Apple 2276
Released: August 26, 1968

'THE BEATLES' ('The White Album')
Apple SWBO 101
Released: November 25, 1968
(Tracks as on UK release; see page 74)

YELLOW SUBMARINE
Apple SW153
Released: January 13, 1969
(Tracks as on UK release; see page 76)

'Get Back'/'Don't Let Me Down'
Apple 2490
Released: May 5, 1969

**'The Ballad of John and Yoko'/'Old Brown
Shoe'**
Apple 2531
Released: June 16, 1969

'Something'/'Come Together'
Apple 2654
Released: October 31, 1969

ABBEY ROAD
Apple SO 383
Released: November 1, 1969
(Tracks as on UK release; see page 80)

HEY JUDE
Apple SW 385
Released: February 26, 1970
Can't Buy Me Love/I Should Have Known
Better/Paperback Writer/Rain/Lady
Madonna/Revolution/Hey Jude/Old
Brown Shoe/Don't Let Me Down/The
Ballad Of John and Yoko

'Let It Be'/'You Know My Name'
Apple 2764
Released: March 2, 1970

**'The Long and Winding Road'/'For You
Blue'**
Apple 2832
Released: May 7, 1970

LET IT BE
Apple ARS 34001
Released: May 15, 1970
(Tracks as on UK release; see page 88)

Above *Examples of 'Beatleg' sleeve design.*

The practice of bootlegging is immoral, illegal and – despite pressures brought to bear by the established recording companies – still very much a flourishing and lucrative business.

Bootlegs enable the insatiable fan to purchase – usually at extortionate prices – rare moments in live performances or hitherto unreleased studio material, broadcasts, demos, out-takes, jam sessions and sweepings from the studio floor which, for one reason or another, have been rejected for commercial release.

Though one or two gems are to be found on bootlegs, the sound quality is invariably of exceedingly poor fidelity, excepting in those very rare instances when subversive sources have gained unauthorised access to the master tapes or acetates.

As will be seen, there is an abundance of Beatlegs but, aside from specific concert recordings and broadcasts, the majority of these 'unofficial' releases are no more than a variation of existing tracks which have been re-cycled and re-processed under other titles. A prime example is the way the innumerable out-takes for the *Let It Be* movie (usually referred to as 'The Get Back Sessions') have been spread exceedingly thin over many albums. Bootlegging bootlegs is now an accepted by-product.

The fact that the Beatles never issued a live album which captured the electrifying atmosphere of Beatlemania at its zenith (though George Martin did, in fact, record a number of shows) has resulted in a brisk under-the-counter trade for those albums – no matter how badly recorded – which feature the group before an audience. Again, most of the songs are duplicated, due to the fact that on stage the Beatles only performed a dozen numbers (most of them hits), but the sheer nostalgic charisma of such concerts makes these albums desirable collectors' items.

Beatlegs are hard to come by and, if buying such product, it is more than probable that one won't be able to preview it before purchase. Therefore, it's a question of 'yer pays yer money and yer takes yer chance'. Whatever the morality and the arguments for and against bootlegs' existence, the fact remains that, with little in the way of overheads and production costs to pay – and definitely nothing in the way of copyrights to be passed on to the artists and composers – the astute bootlegger stands to make anything up to 500 per cent profit on every album sold.

As there are well over sixty Beatlegs in existence, the authors choose to offer a selection.

'Yellow Matter Custard'

I Got a Woman/Glad All Over/I Just Don't Understand/ Slow Down/Please Don't Ever Change/A Shot Of Rhythm and Blues/I'm Sure To Fall/Nothing Shakin' But the Leaves On the Tree/Lonesome Tears In My Eyes/Everyone Wants Someone/I'm Gonna Sit Right Down and Cry Over You/

BOOT LEGS

Crying, Waiting, Hoping/To Know Her Is To Love Her/ Bound By Love

'Out-Takes Vol. 1'

Do You Want to Know a Secret?/You Really Got a Hold On Me/Hippy Hippy Shake/Misery/Money/Till There Was You/From Me To You/Roll Over Beethoven/Love Me Do/ Kansas City/Long Tall Sally/Please Please Me

Rejected versions of commercially released material plus the odd gem like 'Hippy Hippy Shake'.

'Out-Takes Vol. 2'

She Loves You/Words of Love/She's Got the Devil In Her Heart/Anna/Money/There's a Place/Honey Don't/Chains/ I Saw Her Standing There/I'm Sure To Fall/Lucille/Boys

Only thing of interest here is the never-released workout on Little Richard's 'Lucille'.

'Pop Goes the Beatles'

Pop Goes the Beatles/Boys/There's a Place/Lend Me Your Comb/Pop Goes the Beatles/A Shot Of Rhythm and Blues/ Till There Was You/Chains/Twist and Shout/Crying, Waiting, Hoping/Do You Want To Know a Secret?/I'm Gonna Sit Right Down and Cry Over You/Pop Goes the Beatles

Various air-shots (mainly from the BBC) featuring some of their old Star Club and Cavern chestnuts like Arthur Alexander's 'A Shot of Rhythm and Blues'.

'Live At the Paris Olympia. No. 1.'

Twist and Shout/She's a Woman/Ticket To Ride/Can't Buy Me Love/I'm a Loser/ I Wanna Be Your Man/A Hard Day's Night/Baby's In Black/Rock and Roll Music/ Everbody's Trying To Be My Baby/Long Tall Sally

The Beatles' programme from a show they co-headlined with Trini Lopez. French radio apparently have an excellent tape of this concert.

'Live At Shea-1964'

Twist and Shout/All My Loving/She Loves You/Things We Said Today/Roll Over Beethoven/Can't Buy Me Love/If I Fell/I Want To Hold Your Hand/Boys/A Hard Day's Night/Long Tall Sally

'Hollywood Bowl 1964'

Twist and Shout/You Can't Do That/All My Loving/She Loves You/Things We Said Today/Roll Over Beethoven/ Can't Buy Me Love/If I Feel/I Want To Hold Your Hand/ Boys/A Hard Day's Night/Long Tall Sally

George Martin also recorded the Beatles at this venue with an eye to a commercial release. So where is it?

'Tokyo Sixty Six'

Rock and Roll Music/She's a Woman/If I Needed Someone/ Day Tripper/Baby's In Black/I Feel Fine/Yesterday/I Wanna Be Your Man/Nowhere Man/Paperback Writer/ I'm Down

It's the same in any language. One of their last expeditions into the concert arena.

'Kum Back'

Get Back/When You Walk/Let It Be/One After 909/Teddy Boy/Two Of Us/Don't Let Me Down/I've Got a Feeling/ The Long and Winding Road/Dig It/For You Blue/Dig a Pony/Get Back

Basically, the main ingredients for all 'Let It Be' bootlegs. 'Teddy Boy' re-appeared on the 'McCartney' album, while 'The Long and Winding Road' is free from Phil Spector's suffocating violins and choir.

'Cinelogue'

Piano Intro/Don't Let Me Down/Maxwell's Silver Hammer/ Two Of Us/I've Got a Feeling/Oh, Darling/One After 909/ Piano Boogie/Two Of Us/Across The Universe/Dig a Pony/

Suzy Parker/Besame Mucho/I Me Mine/For You Blue/ Octopus's Garden/You've Really Got a Hold On Me/The

Long and Winding Road/Shake, Rattle and Roll/Kansas City/Lawdy Miss Clawdy/Dig It/Get Back/Let It Be/For You Blue/Don't Let Me Down

The entire 'Let It Be' movie soundtrack spread over two albums.

'The Beatles Complete Christmas Collection: 1963–1969'
– The Beatles Fan Club Christmas records
By way of a personal gesture to the members of their fan club the Beatles used to record a special 'members-only' disc which was distributed free of charge to their paid-up fans. Beatle lunacy and sometimes a snippet or two of music prevails on these endearing little curios.

'The Never Released Mary Jane'
What's the New Mary Jane?/Shout/Interview/People Say/ You Know My Name/Long Tall Sally/A Hard Day's Night/ Things We Said Today/I'm Walking/Sie Liebt Dich

'Have You Heard the Word?'
Have You Heard the Word?/You Really Got a Hold On Me/ The Long and Winding Road (reggae)/Maxwell's Silver Hammer/Whole Lotta Shakin'/Octopus's Garden/I Me Mine/Don't Let Me Down/I Forgot To Remember/Twist and Shout/Roll Over Beethoven/Long Tall Sally/Dizzy Miss Lizzy/Lucille

'Spicy Beatles Songs – What's the New Mary Jane? – A Lurid Tale of Lusts and Weakness!!'
Have You Heard the Word?/Don't Let Me Down/Those Were the Days/What's the New Mary Jane/Cottonfields/ Twist and Shout/Dizzy Miss Lizzy/You Really Got a Hold On Me/Roll Over Beethoven/All My Loving/I Wanna Be Your Man/A Hard Day's Night/Things We Said Today/ From Us To You.
Demos and broadcasts plus a send-up of Mary Hopkins' 'Those Were the Days'.

'Abbey Road Revisited – Those Were the Days'
You Really Got a Hold On Me/Have You Heard the Word?/ Don't Let Me Down/Those Were the Days/Mean Mr Mustard/Kenny Everett Jingle/Step Inside Love/Cotton Fields/Twist and Shout/Dizzy Miss Lizzy/From Me To You/ Twist and Shout/This Boy/I Saw Her Standing There/She Loves You/I Want To Hold Your Hand/Please Please Me/ All My Loving
A selection of out-takes, jokes, demos and airshots.

'Renaissance Minstrels No. 1.'
From Me To You/Twist and Shout/This Boy/I Saw Her Standing There/She Loves You (1)/I Want To Hold Your Hand/Please Please Me/All My Loving/She Loves You (2)
The Ed Sullivan TV shows.

'The Great Rock 'n' Roll Circus'
Yer Blues Jam – John Lennon, Eric Clapton, Keith Richard and Mitch Mitchell
Culled from the never-released 'Rolling Stones Rock & Roll Circus' movie. The other cuts feature The Who and various odds and ends.

'John Lennon & Yoko Ono/One-To-One'
Mother/We're All Water/Imagine/Come Together/Give Peace a Chance/Attica State/Sisters Oh Sisters/The Luck of the Irish
John and Yoko captured at various American benefit rallies.

'John Lennon/Chuck Berry Telecasts'
John Sinclair/It's Hard To Wait/The Luck Of the Irish Sisters Oh Sisters/We All Woke Up/Woman Is the Nigger Of the World/Attica State/Johnny B. Goode/Memphis/ Shake It/Sakura/Imagine

'Paul McCartney & Wings Live'
Big Barn Bed/My Little Woman/My Love/The Mess/Maybe I'm Amazed/Long Tall Sally/Another Day/Hi, Hi, Hi/Oh

Woman Oh Why/Gotta Sing, Gotta Dance/Live and Let Die/Bluebird/Michelle/Heart Of the Country/Yesterday

'James Paul McCartney – TV Special'
Uncle Albert/My Love/Maybe I'm Amazed/Big Barn Bed/ My Little Woman/The Mess/Long Tall Sally/Another Day/ Oh Woman Oh Why/Hi, Hi, Hi/Gotta Sing, Gotta Dance/ Mary Had a Little Lamb/Bluebird-Michelle-Heart Of the Country Medley/Yesterday

'Supertracks' – Ed Sullivan Show '66'
Paperback Writer/Rain/I should Have Known Better/ If I Fell/ And I love Her/Tell Me Why/Peace Of Mind/Let It Be/ Hey Jude

'Sunday Night at The London Palladium and Blackpool Night Out TV Shows'
Please Mr Postman/All My Loving/I Wanna Be Your Man/ Till There Was You/Please Mr Postman (2)/I Want To Hold Your Hand/Comedy Sketch with Mike and Bernie Winters/
I Want To Hold Your Hand/This Boy/All My Loving/ Money/Twist and Shout

Above *Artwork for a record that was never made.*

'The Beatles'
Till There Was You/I Want To Hold Your Hand/This Boy/ All My Loving/Yesterday/Nowhere Man/She's a Woman/ Everybody's Trying To Be My Baby/Rock and Roll Music/ I Feel Fine/Ticket To Ride/Johnny B. Goode/Memphis Tennessee/Some Other Guy/You Really Got a Hold On Me/Shout

'Cavern Club – 1964'
Medley: Love Me Do – Please Please Me – From Me To You/She Loves You/I Want To Hold Your Hand/Can't Buy Me Love/Long Tall Sally/She Loves You/Act Naturally/ Can't Buy Me Love/Baby's In Black/Help!/I'm Down/ Twist and Shout/I Feel Fine/Dizzy Miss Lizzy/Ticket To Ride

'Top Of the Pops'
People Say/I'm Walking/Hey Jude/Revolution/Long Tall Sally/A Hard Day's Night/Things We Said Today/Shout/ Twist and Shout/You Can't Do That/All My Loving/She Loves You/Things We Said Today/Roll Over Beethoven/ Sie Liebt Dich/Some Other Guy

ODDS & ENDS

'Komm Gib Mir Deine Hand'/'Sie Liebt Dich'
(German) Odeon 22671
To say the least, German ain't a good language to rock in but by way of a personal gesture, the Beatles did their best with 'I Want To Hold Your Hand' and 'She Loves You' rendered into the Teutonic tongue.

These tracks were issued in America but never in England.

'If I Fell'/'Tell Me Why'
Parlophone DP 562
This was Made In England for Harold Wilson's mid-'sixties White Heat export drive to Europe; enterprising British record dealers re-imported quantities of this single – which explains the Parlophone label and the out-of-sequence catalogue number.

'The Hollywood Bowl Concert'
Twist and Shout/She's a Woman/I Feel Fine/Ticket To Ride/Everybody's Trying To Be My Baby/Can't Buy Me Love/Baby's In Black/I Wanna Be Your Man/A Hard Day's Night/Help!/I'm Down
Recorded on the spot (August 29, 1965) by George Martin. this could have been the Beatles first 'live' album. A couple of years ago, there were persistent rumours that Apple were going to release these concert recordings as a memento. Nothing has been heard since.

George Martin also recorded the Beatles at Carnegie Hall on Feb 7, 1964.

'Beatles Hamburg Tape'
Be-Bop-a-Lula/I Saw Her Standing There/Hallelujah! I Love Her So/My Girl Is Red Hot/Shimmy Shimmy/Red Sails In the Sunset/Nothin' Shakin' But the Leaves On the Tree/Little Queenie/Long Tall Sally/Till There Was You/A Taste Of Honey/Falling In Love Again/I Remember You/Ask Me Why/Your Feet's Too Big/Besame Mucho/To Know Her Is To Love Her/Roll Over Beethoven/Sweet Little Sixteen/Everybody's Trying To Be My Baby/I'm Gonna Sit Right Down and Cry Over You/Talkin' 'Bout You/Mr Moonlight/Matchbox/Roll Over Beethoven (alternate take)
This interesting collection of tracks was recorded by Teddy 'Kingsize' Taylor at the Star Club, Hamburg, after Pete Best had left and before 'Love Me Do' had broken. It is reputed to be of excellent quality – yet it is significant that, at the time of writing, no major record company (including EMI/Apple) has seen fit to issue the many collectors' items available on this tape.

'Decca Records Audition Tape'
Red Sails In the Sunset/To Know Her Is To Love Her/Memphis, Tennessee/The Sheik Of Araby/Three Cool Cats/Please Mr Postman/Money/Till There Was You/Like Dreamers Do/Hello Little Girl/Love Of the Loved
This session took place on January 1, 1962. Decca Records turned them down and have been apologising ever since.

Some of these tracks, plus 'Your Feet's Too Big', 'Love Me Do' and 'P.S. I Love You' were re-recorded on the later audition tape they made for EMI Records.
EMI signed them and have been boasting ever since.

A scant few of these songs have crept on to various bootlegs.

Rock 'n' roll oldies recorded during the 'Let It Be' sessions
Stand By Me/Baby, I Don't Care/Thirty Days/Hippy Hippy Shake/Short Fat Fanny/A Fool Like Me/You Win Again/Turn Around/Blue Suede Shoes/True Love/The Right String But the Wrong Yo Yo/Sure To Fall/Memphis. Tennessee/Maybelline/Johnny B. Goode/Sweet Little Sixteen/Little Queenie/Roll Over Beethoven/Rock and Roll Music/Singing the Blues/The Midnight Special/Michael Row the Boat Ashore/Devil In Her Heart/Hitchhike/Money/Three Cool Cats/Good Rockin' Tonight/All Shook Up/Don't Be Cruel/Lucille/Send Me Some Lovin'/Dizzy Miss Lizzy/Be-Bop-a-Lula/Save the Last Dance For Me/Besame Mucho/A Lotta Lovin'/The House Of the Rising Sun/Tea For Two/Blowin' In the Wind/I Shall Be Released/All Along the Watchtower/High Heeled Sneakers/It's Only Make Believe/C'mon Everybody/Somethin' Else/Bad Boy/The Rock Island Line/Third Man Theme/Piece Of My Heart/It's So Easy/Oh My Soul/Lawdy Miss Clawdy/Some Other Guy/Kansas City/You Really Got a Hold On Me/Shake Rattle and Roll/Stairway To Paradise/Carol/Lend Me Your Comb/She Said, She Said/You Can't Do That/Whole Lotta Shakin' Goin' On/Love Me Do

---

Like all professional musicians, the individual Beatles have. from time to time, made guest appearances either as featured sidemen, back-up vocalists or producers on recorded material for artists with whom they have strong affinities: Leon Russell, Stephen Stills, James Taylor, Carly Simon, Bob Dylan, Eric Clapton, Gary Wright, Peter Frampton, Billy Preston, Mary Hopkins, the Radha Krishna Temple, Doris Troy, Ravi Shankar, Jackie Lomax, Alvin Lee, Tony Ashton, Harry Nilsson, David Peel, Badfinger and the Rolling Stones. Nevertheless, there are certain extra-curricular activities which, fortunately, we feel able to document.

'Badge' from 'Goodbye' by Cream
Polydor 583053
Produced: Felix Pappalardi
Co-written by Eric Clapton and George Harrison, the latter also plays rhythm guitar under one of his many bizarre pseudonyms, L'Angelo Misterioso.

'My Dark Hour' from 'Brave New World' by Steve Miller
Capitol E-ST 184
Produced: Glyn Johns
This track is the result of a studio jam that took place at Olympic studios around the time of 'Let It Be'. After the participants had left (one at a time), the two last remaining musicians – Steve Miller and Paul McCartney – decided to record a song together. Adopting the Silver Beatles pseudonym of Paul Ramon, McCartney played bass and drums, Miller guitar, and both collaborated on the vocal track – Miller taking the lead.

'The Family Way' (soundtrack)
Decca SKL 4847
Produced: George Martin
Paul McCartney's first attempt to write soundtrack music. Unmemorable music for a twee North Country story.

'Tommy' The London Symphony Orchestra and Guest Soloists.
A&M Records SP 99001
Produced: Lou Reizner
In Lou Reizner's gargantuan production of Pete Townshend's celebrated rock opera, Ringo is cast in the role of Uncle Ernie (the child molestor). Like most of Ringo's film parts, an adequate cameo role. For the Rainbow Theatre charity galas, Ringo was replaced by Keith Moon and Vivian Stanshall.

'Try Some, Buy Some'/'Tandoori Chicken' by Ronnie Spector
Apple 33
Produced: Phil Spector and George Harrison
To mark the comeback to active recording of Phil Spector's wife Ronnie (lead singer of the Ronettes and perhaps the most accomplished girl singer of the early 'sixties), Spector burdened her with this somewhat ponderous and tuneless Harrison song. Phil Spector desperately wanted this to be a hit but, as Ronnie later revealed, she didn't like the song from the beginning and so her heart wasn't in it. Needless to say, it bombed.

'God Save Us'/'Do the Oz' by Bill Elliott and the Plastic Oz Band
Apple 36
Produced: John Lennon, Yoko Ono, Mal Evans and Phil Spector
Composed specifically by the Yoco-Lennons as a fund-raiser for the defence during the infamous Oz magazine Old Bailey obscenity trial. Although credited to Bill Elliott and the Electric Oz Band everybody knew it was Lennon (he and Yoko subsequently marched in the Oz demo). Harmless dialectic. It didn't sell.

'Son of Dracula' (soundtrack)
Rapple APL 1–0220
Produced: Harry Nilsson and Richard Perry
Ringo plays occasional drums and Merlin, Nilsson sings occasional songs and grabs the title role. Both participate in predictable dialogue.

'Have You Heard the Word?'/'Futting, the Futz'
Beacon 160
It would take Sherlock Holmes to get to the bottom of this, a Great Unknown Beatles Mystery. Hardly any concrete evidence can be attributed to this deleted single, which allegedly features Lennon and some of the Bee Gees. The fact that it has appeared in bootleg form adds some weight to the myth but still doesn't separate fact from fiction.

TONY SHERIDAN AND THE BEATLES

'My Bonnie'/'The Saints'*
Polydor 66 833
Produced: Bert Kaempfert
Released: June 1963

'Sweet Georgia Brown'*/'Nobody's Child'*
Polydor 52 906
Produced: Bert Kaempfert
Released: January 1964

'Cry For a Shadow'/'Why'***
Polydor 52 275
Produced: Bert Kaempfert
Released: March 1964

'Ain't She Sweet'*/'Take Out Some Insurance On Me Baby'***
Polydor 52 317
Produced: Bert Kaempfert
Released: May 1964

* Tony Sheridan – vocal, Beatles – backing
** Beatles instrumental
*** John Lennon – vocal, Beatles – backing

124

PETE BEST

In the halcyon days of Beatlemania, get-rich-quick artists scoured the back streets of Liverpool for someone – anyone – who might have had the remotest connection with the Beatles.

Tony Sheridan, by far the most talented of these, was the first to be exploited. Pete Best, the Beatles' dethroned drummer, was the Number Two seed – but, unfortunately, the Beatles' decision to fire him had some musical justification.

One ridiculous attempt to enshrine him was made by Decca ('I'm Gonna Knock On Your Door' – Decca F 11929) – but it was left to the Americans to carry the sorry process to the usual ludicrous extremes. Best was tonsorially mutated from his James Dean look into a second-hand Beatle. Several crummy pictures were taken; several painfully inferior tracks were hurriedly recorded; the whole sordid package was issued under the misleading title of **'Best Of the Beatles'** (Savage Records BM 71).

Reaching its nadir when a double-sided cover version of the Beatles' 'Kansas City' and 'Boys' (Cameo 391) – the latter being Ringo's showcase at the time – were released as the ultimate 'cash-in'. Other records followed, but to little avail.

This whole episode was most unsavoury and Pete Best failed to profit in any way from the experience.

Right *John and Yoko at the Oz demo.*

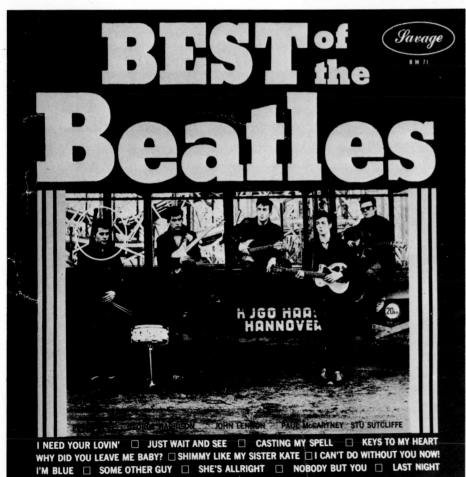

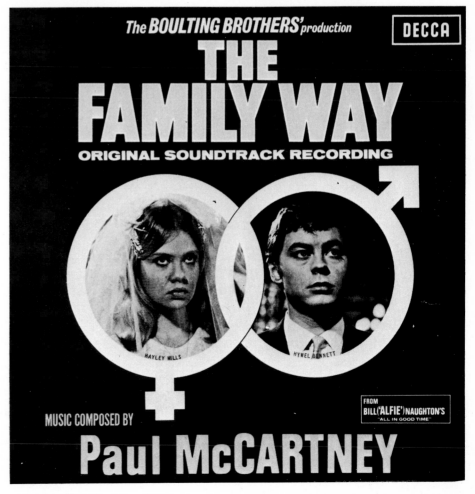

FELLOW TRAVELLERS

Where would Peter and Gordon, Billy J. Kramer and The Fourmost be without more than a little Help From Their Friends Lennon, Harrison and McCartney? All these tracks were composed by said Lennon, Harrison and McCartney and, except for a few, remained commercially unrecorded by the Beatles.

Billy J. Kramer and the Dakotas:
'Do You Want To Know a Secret?'/'I'll Be On My Way'
Parlophone R 5023
'Bad To Me'/'I Call Your Name'
Parlophone R 5049
'I'll Keep You Satisfied'
Parlophone R 5073
'From a Window'
Parlophone R 5156

The Fourmost:
'Hello Little Girl'
Parlophone R 5056
'I'm In Love'
Parlophone R 5078

Peter and Gordon:
'World Without Love'
Columbia DB 7225
'Nobody I Know'
Columbia DB 7292
'I Don't Want To See You Again'
Columbia DB 7356
'Woman'
Columbia DB 7834

Cilla Black:
'Love Of the Loved'
Parlophone R 5056
'It's For You'
Parlophone R 5162
'Step Inside Love'
Parlophone R 5674

Mary Hopkin:
'Goodbye'
Apple 10

The Applejacks:
'Like Dreamers Do'
Decca F 11916

P. J. Proby:
'That Means a Lot'
Liberty LIB 10125

The Strangers:
'One and One Is Two'
Philips BF 1335

The Rolling Stones:
'I Wanna Be Your Man'
Decca F 11764

Tommy Quickly:
'Tip Of My Tongue'
Piccadilly 7N 35137

Chris Barber:
'Catcall'
Marmalade 598 005

Badfinger:
'Come and Get It'
Apple 4 20

The Black Dyke Mills Band:
'Thingumybob'
Apple 4

John Christie:
'4th Of July'
Polydor 2058 496

Peggy Lee
'Let's Love'
Atlantic K 50064
(Also available as a single K 10527)

Scaffold
'Liverpool Lou'/'Ten Years After On Strawberry Jam'
Warner Bros K 16400

Mike McGear
'Leave It'/'Sweet Baby'
Warner Bros K 16446

Mike McGear
'McGear'
Warner Bros K 56051
Sea Breeze/What Do We Really Know (Paul McCartney)/Norton (Paul McCartney–Mike McGear)/Leave It (Paul and Linda McCartney)/Have You Got Problems? (Paul McCartney–Mike McGear)/The Casket (Paul McCartney–Roger McGough)/Rainbow Lady (Paul McCartney–Mike McGear)/Simply Love You (Paul McCartney–Mike McGear)/Givin' Grease a Ride (Paul McCartney–Mike McGear)/The Man Who Found God On the Moon (Paul McCartney–Mike McGear)

The Country Hams
'Walking In The Park With Eloise'/'Bridge On The River Suite'
EMI 2220

Rod Stewart
'Mine For Me' from 'Smiler'
Mercury 9104 001

Harry Nilsson
'Mucho Mungo' and 'Mt Elga'
from 'Pussy Cats'
RCA APL 1 0570

Johnny Winter
'Rock and Roll People'
from 'John Dawson Winter III'
SKY 80586

Jackie Lomax
'Sour Milk Sea'
from 'Is This What You Want'
Apple SAPCOR 6
(Also available as a single Apple 3.)

Doris Troy
'Ain't That Cute?'
Apple SAPCOR 13
Produced: Doris Troy
Ain't That Cute? (George Harrison–Doris Troy)/Special Care/Give Me Back My Dynamite (George Harrison–Doris Troy)/You Tore Me Up Inside/Games People Play/Gonna Get My Baby Back (George Harrison–Doris Troy–Richard Starkey–Stephen Stills)/I've Got To Be Strong/Hurry/So Far/Exactly Like You/You Give Me Joy Joy (George Harrison–Doris Troy–Richard Starkey–Stephen Stills)/Don't Call Me No More/Jacob's Ladder (Trad Arr: George Harrison–Doris Troy)
N.B. 'Ain't That Cute?' available as a single Apple 24.
'Jacob's Ladder' available as a single Apple 28

Billy Preston
'Sing One For The Lord'
from 'Encouraging Words'
Apple SAPCOR 14

Alvin Lee and Mylon LeFevre
'So Sad (No Love Of His Own)'
from 'On The Road To Freedom'
Chrysalis CHR 1054

Ron Wood
'Far East Man'
from 'I've Got My Own Album To Do'
Warner Bros K 56065

ALL ABOARD THE BEATLE BANDWAGON
'I'm Better Than the Beatles' – Brad Berwick and the Bugs
'My Boyfriend Got a Beatle Haircut' – Donna Lynn
'The Beatle Flying Saucer' – Ed Solomon
'Frankenstein Meets the Beatles' – Jekyll and Hyde
'The Beatles' Barber' – Scott Douglas
'I Love You Ringo' – Bonnie Jo Mason [Cher Bono]
'Beatle Beat' – Ella Fitzgerald
'I Hate the Beatles' – Allan Sherman
'Saga of the Beatles' – Johnny and the Hurricanes
'I want To Kiss Ringo Goodbye' – Penny Valentine
'A Beatle I Want To Be' – Sonny Curtis
'Beatle Crazy' – Bill Clifton
'We Love the Beatles' (Beatlemania) – the Vernons Girls
'I Want To Be a Beatle' – Gene Cornish and the Unbeetables
'All I Want For Christmas Is a Beatle' – Dora Bryan
'Yes, You Can Hold My Hand' – The Beatlettes
'Beatle Fever' – Brett and Terry
'The Beatle Dance' – Ernie Maresca
'Yeah, Yeah' – The Bedbugs
'Ringo For President' – Rolf Harris
'The Boy With the Beatle Hair' – The Swans
'We Love You Beatles' – The Carefrees
'John, Paul, George and Ringo' – The Bulldogs
'Sing a Song Of Beatles' – Dick James
'Ain't No Beatle' – Gary Sanders

UNASHAMED CASH-INS
(RECORDED BEATLERAMA)

'Hear The Beatles Tell All'
Vee-Jay V-J Promo 202

'All About The Beatles – Answered By Louise Harrison Caldwell'
Recar Records 2012

'Live Beatlemania Concert' by Ed Rudy
Radio Pulsebeat News Records Vol. 1

'The American Beatles Tour' by Ed Rudy
Radio Pulsebeat News Records Vol. 2

'Beatles Blast In Shea Stadium' described by Erupting Fans
Audio Journal Records

Opposite page A group of 'fellow travellers', who used songs composed by, but not recorded by the Beatles, and one example of an 'unashamed cash-in' (top right). Left to right: Badfinger, The Fourmost, Peter and Gordon (Peter is Peter Asher, Jane's brother), Cilla Black, Tommy Quickly and P. J. Proby.

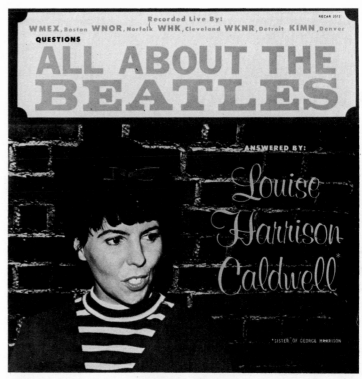

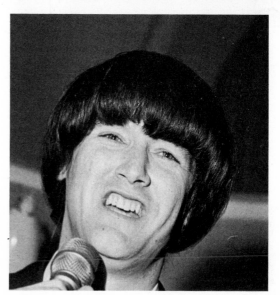

Reader's diary of
further Beatle events.
To be filled in
as and when . . .